*A Year of
Trading Spaces*

DISCARD

by Paige Davis

Paige by
Paige

Meredith® Books
Des Moines, Iowa

Meredith® Press
An imprint of Meredith® Books

Paige by Paige: *A Year of Trading Spaces*
Editor: Vicki L. Ingham
Senior Associate Design Director: Mick Schnepf
Copy Chief: Terri Fredrickson
Copy and Production Editor: Victoria Forlini
Editorial Operations Manager: Karen Schirm
Managers, Book Production: Pam Kvitne, Marjorie J. Schenkelberg, Rick von Holdt
Contributing Copy Editor: Stacey Schildroth
Contributing Proofreaders: Heidi Johnson, Gretchen Kauffman, Margaret Smith
Electronic Production Coordinator: Paula Forest
Editorial and Design Assistants: Kaye Chabot, Karen McFadden, Mary Lee Gavin

Meredith® Books
Editor in Chief: Linda Raglan Cunningham
Design Director: Matt Strelecki
Executive Editor, Home Decorating and Design: Denise L. Caringer

Publisher: James D. Blume
Executive Director, Marketing: Jeffrey Myers
Executive Director, New Business Development: Todd M. Davis
Executive Director, Sales: Ken Zagor
Director, Operations: George A. Susral
Director, Production: Douglas M. Johnston
Business Director: Jim Leonard

Vice President and General Manager: Douglas J. Guendel

Meredith Publishing Group
President, Publishing Group: Stephen M. Lacy
Vice President-Publishing Director: Bob Mate

Meredith Corporation
Chairman and Chief Executive Officer: William T. Kerr

In Memoriam: E. T. Meredith III (1933–2003)

Cover Photograph: Gideon Lewin

First and foremost I want to thank the amazingly talented and dedicated cast and crew of <u>Trading Spaces</u>: Eddie Barnard, Frank Bielec, Larry Blasé, Cyndi Butz, Ron Cornwall, Denise Cramsey, Patrick Denzer, Natalie Feldman, Jeff Fender, Gary Folsom, Mark Gambol, Genevieve Gorder, Daniel Hawkes, Mindy Karp, Aimee Kramer, Kevin Maraza, Rob Marish, Andy Obeck, Tim Obeck, Amy Wynn Pastor, Ty Pennington, Kelle Rogers, Hildi Santo Tomás, Jeff Schirmer, Steven Schwartz, Laurie Smith, Kia Steave-Dickerson, Laura Swalm, Jeff Wager, Edward Walker, Doug Wilson, Vern Yip, and all the local crew who cared for and loved our show as much as we do. You have been an inspiration to me every day. The more I wrote about you and our experiences together, the more in awe of you I became. I admire and respect each and every one of you more than I can possibly express.

The Neighbors — the bravest, most interesting, and fun group of people I've had the pleasure of knowing. You are stars now too, especially in my eyes.

PJ Mark — Well, I achieved my goal. Now I know what it's like to write a book and see it published. Thank you for holding my hand each step of the way. Your support, patience, and sympathetic ear saved me more times than was warranted. You are a gem.

Kim Gieske — Hey girl, none of this craziness would have even happened if you hadn't taken the initiative to introduce me to PJ. Thanks for all you did to help this book come to fruition.

The folks at TLC/Discovery and Banyan Productions who answered all my questions and were a support behind the scenes as I was writing, especially: Mary Beth Anderson, Chantal Bucolo, Tom Farrell, Harvey, Chloe Kanter, Marc Lowenstein, Michele Monte, Susan Murrow, and Susan Witte.

Vicki Ingham - You were the light at the end of the tunnel. (You even blinded me a couple of times.) I felt confident when I was working with you. You convinced me everything was going to be all right. I am indebted to you for your guidance and clear vision.

Mick Schnepf - Dude, the pages look awesome. I know it wasn't easy. Thank you for bringing my book to life.

Matt Strelecki — In the midst of all your own responsibilities, you took on so many of mine, and in the process we became great friends. You are my hero.

Jeff Schirmer, Kenny Fried, Michael Aguilera, Thea Samuels, and all who contributed pictures to these pages. You rock.

Patrick, my love — Your unwavering support has given me strength so many times, and this past season has been no exception. "You are that rare and awesome thing . . ."

1

It's hard to believe that less than a year ago I was at this exact same place: on the brink of a new season of <u>Trading Spaces</u>. So much has changed! Back then, I never could have anticipated the twists and turns of my on- and off-camera journeys and the dramatic changes to my life as the show skyrocketed in popularity.

As I sit here in my Upper West Side apartment with my bags packed, I can't wait to embark on another season of laughter, tears, joys, and tension. Last season was incredible. I learned that every conceivable emotion resides in homes all over America. And these emotions are just waiting to be expressed on our show. It's amazing how personal this process becomes for our participants, even though it's "just a room."

I haven't seen members of the cast and crew for a couple of months, so tomorrow will be a cascade of reunions. I look forward to the friendships that we will inevitably forge as we welcome new additions to our family—in front of the camera and behind the scenes.

Other big changes are already underway for us, but the basics will stay the same: We'll still have homeowners, designers, and carpenters working to put together rooms in just two days with a budget of only $1,000. Oh yeah, and me: I'll still be there witnessing it all.

© Marc Jeff Schirmer

Day 1: Cumberland, Maine
Designers: Genevieve & Doug
Neighbors: Joyce & Steve and Ellen & Darryl

According to Genevieve, Maine is the largest exporter of toothpicks. Do you think that's a statistic for the whole world or just the United States? Hmm.

9:00 a.m.

It's so cold today that I had to dig out a wool sweater from the bottom of my suitcase. *(The Mainers keep telling us this weather isn't seasonal.)* Normally I wouldn't bring so many personal clothes with me, but I schlepped this stuff along because I'm meeting my husband, Patrick, after we shoot this batch of episodes in the Portland area. He's an actor, traveling with the national stage tour of The Lion King, so when I'm free, I go where he is.

We usually show up on the set at 8:00 on our first morning of shooting, and the Key Swap takes place around 9:00. We're off to a good start: The homeowners are already having a great time. No need to break the ice with these folks—it's broken. As they joke with the crew, the couples show they can dish it out as well as they can take it. Ellen applied to the show without telling her husband, Darryl, or the other couple, Joyce and Steve. She didn't think anything would come of it. *(We hear that from a lot of people. They write to us but assume they'll never get chosen.)* Joyce and Ellen are sisters, and brother-in-law Steve is hinting about paybacks. They tease each other mercilessly; Joyce even pulled the old "Let me get that for ya, Hon" routine and swatted an imaginary fly off Steve by smacking him on the head.

3:43 p.m.

I've been running back and forth between the two homes,

4

monitoring the progress. The houses are a little farther apart than we normally allow on the show *(a three-minute walk, max)*, but it's barely a 60-second drive. Getting in and out of the car is the name of the game today.

I expected those first-day-of-school jitters, but it feels more like we never left for the hiatus—everyone is back in the swing of things. That's good. It proves we have the mechanics of the show down cold, even with some new faces around. We have two new associate producers coming aboard. I met Mindy yesterday, and from what I can tell she seems pretty excited about her new job. On the next shoot I'll get to meet Kevin, the second AP, and Cyndi, who will alternate cities with Patrick as our location coordinator. It will be interesting to see how these new folks affect the dynamic of our group. I firmly believe that the closeness of our cast and crew has contributed to the show's growing success and popularity. We're a tight-knit group, and the strength of Trading Spaces blossomed out of our collective fierce commitment to give 100%. Our crew is full of martyrs, all of them striving to be the one who works the hardest. Behind the scenes there's a constant chorus of: "I'll get it!" "I'll do it!" "I'll take care of it!" and "I'm on it!"

Big drama of the day: *When they loaded the trailer to come to Portland, they accidentally left behind many of the tools and supplies we need. Suddenly we realized there wasn't a set of pliers, a staple gun, a glue gun, or a screwdriver to be had. As location coordinator, Patrick came to the rescue. Talk about an emergency trip to the home improvement store! Whew!*

6:58 p.m.

The teams have their homework assignments. Looks like there's not much for me to help with, so I'm heading back to the hotel.

Later...

I was craving a great seafood dinner tonight, something you'd think I'd be able to find in Maine, of all places. You ever have a shrimp that tastes and feels like a cooked potato? That's what my dinner tasted like. I hope I don't get sick. The people working at the hotel suggested the restaurant, saying we just had to go there. We should have known what we were in for when we saw it was a floating restaurant.

Note to self: *That's code for tourist trap!*

* *June 17th, 2002*
Day 2

2:30 p.m.
Knocked out the Open for this episode. (The Open is the introduction segment, when I tell where we are.) The sound guys

were frustrated with my jacket because the snaps jingled and my microphone picked it up when I moved around. Oops. Guess I won't be wearing this jacket again. No more noisy wardrobe. "No more wire hangers!"

3:30 p.m.

The neighbors are getting comfortable with the camera. I think we have a couple of actors in our midst. It's fun when the participants ham it up. I love the transformation that happens with many of our homeowners. On the first day, during the initial interviews, they feel awkward in front of the camera, but by the end of the second day they're ready to go out and get an agent. One guy (who was extremely nervous at the start of the show) even began telling us how to edit our footage as we were shooting him. He'd say things like, "You guys can use this for a bumper shot." It's wonderful to watch folks loosen up. It means they're enjoying themselves and that we're helping them feel comfortable.

12:38 a.m.

The Reveals (*the part of the show when I take the couples in to see their finished rooms*) went well. As I anticipated, Joyce was disappointed that we painted over her wallpaper. I wish we had been able to cover that issue on camera earlier in the day, but there just wasn't time to fit it in. I think Doug pounced on this opportunity to refute the notion that you can't paint over wallpaper. On the other hand, in Genevieve's house, they removed the wallpaper from the walls to be painted because she said it wasn't right to paint over it. It would be interesting to hear the two designers address that issue, but it's hard to fit everything in when you're editing two days into an hour-long show.

Our first episode went off without a hitch, even with the tool fiasco. Maybe it's a sign. Last season our first episode didn't wrap until 12:30 a.m.! It's 12:38 a.m. right now, but this time around I've already had dinner and drinks with the gang.

Vern arrived this evening in time to meet up with us. Yay! It was fantastic to hang out. Once again, we went to a local place for a fish dinner and, once again, I managed to miss out on getting a fabulous seafood meal. I'm beginning to think I should add this talent to my resume: the uncanny ability to pick the absolute worst place to eat. My choices were limited, though. Everything closes around here at 9:00 p.m.! What's up with that? *Toto, we're not in Manhattan anymore.*

Doug and Genevieve headed back to Manhattan tonight. Doug has to catch a flight to Paris tomorrow. He's going to France to attend Hildi's wedding. I wish I could be there, but the shooting schedule marches on.....

*June 18th, 2002
Day Off

It was not a day off for Vern and me; we did a few radio interviews this morning. The day got off to a dubious start as we wandered around the hotel parking garage looking for each other. The mishaps just grew from there. We got lost on our way to the radio station. I checked the directions before we left, but I trusted they would make more sense when we were in the car. I was wrong. Eventually I called the radio station to ask for help. The DJ exclaimed, *"Oooh, you're coming from that part of town?! Yep, those are the wrong directions. Sorry."* He got us turned around, and actually we didn't wind up going very far out of the way. We made it to the station on time. We rock.

After the interview I rode around with Vern to look for a cheap sofa for the room he'll be working on in the next episode. (*The designers see pictures of their rooms before they arrive in each city.*) We tried a few places—a vintage shop and Goodwill—but we found our gem at the Salvation Army. We knew the Salvation Army was our last shot, so Vern was about to settle on a sofa that he thought was his only choice. We asked the manager if we could look in the back room, but she said, "No way, only employees can go back there." She checked the back for us and said there weren't any other sofas. Vern was really hoping to find something that he liked better, but when you're at a thrift store, working on a time limit, you really can't be choosy. He bought the $60 sofa and we loaded it into his SUV. We were about to drive away when the manager came running outside to tell us she finally realized why we looked familiar to her: "You're on Trading Spaces!" Next thing we knew, we were in the back room, looking at items that weren't ready for the main floor yet. Sure enough, Vern spotted a much better sofa option and a storage unit he could use as a console table behind the sofa. He scored! The second sofa was one-third the price of the first one. *I picked up a pair of antique ice tongs for Genevieve. I thought she could use them in a room someday. I can't wait to tell her!*

The Salvation Army was remarkable. Seeing the inner operations of this place was like touring a factory. There was quite an assembly line of sorting, folding, and organizing. They even had a bin for rejects. Those items went through a gigantic compactor to be pressed just like junk cars and packed between sheets of cardboard. It was like a cartoon. Vern loaded the $20 sofa into his SUV and made arrangements to pick up the storage chest tomorrow. Mission accomplished.

We got lost driving back to the hotel too! Can you believe it? At one point we drove the wrong way down a one-way street! A few people honked and one woman kind of yelled. Good grief. We did

9

make it back safely, but barely.

By the time we got back, Laurie had made it in. She is radiant—pregnancy suits her. The doctor said she's having a textbook pregnancy. Of course she is. It's Laurie. She wouldn't have it any other way. It would be like Martha Stewart setting a table without coordinating napkins. Everyone is trying to guess if she'll have a boy or a girl. I'm guessing a girl. No, a boy. No, a girl. Oh, I don't know. She's carrying very high. What does that mean again?

* June 20th, 2002

Day 1: Portland, Maine
Designers: Vern & Laurie
Neighbors: Jeanne & Jim and Laura & Scott

More press. All the reporters want the same thing: live shots. They don't want anything "staged." This guy from the Portland Press Herald said he wanted to capture the homeowners when they were working and the cameras were rolling, to get "real shots." Well, guess what? We don't let any photographer take pictures when the camera is rolling. The microphones would pick up the sound of the shutter and the flash would show up on our tape. Sorry. I feel bad in a way, because I know they're trying to get the coolest shot they can get, but they have to keep in mind that we're trying to complete two rooms and create a television show in a very limited amount of time.

10:00 a.m.

We've got two, count them, **two** pregnant women on our teams today. There's Laurie, of course, and one of the homeowners, Laura, is also going to have a baby. She's seven months along. At least they're not on the same team. If they were, we'd never finish the room. At one point they were each banished from their homes because of toxic fumes from oil-based primer. I pulled out the Paige Cam to talk with them while they were hanging out together. It is dangerous to let teammates from opposite households chat with each other, I tell ya! Laurie almost spilled the beans about one of the projects in her house. Luckily, she caught herself before she said too much. It was so funny to see her eyes bug out and watch the words crash inside her mouth as she caught herself. We all laughed so hard. Party over! I made them go back to their own homes so there was no chance of another slipup. We take the secrecy issue very seriously, but it can be really tricky. You can never let your guard down.

10:55 a.m.

In Vern's room they're putting tin tiles on the ceiling. He told the homeowners that the tile edges were very sharp and gave them gloves to wear. Unfortunately while Laura was waiting for the camera guys to set up, she accidentally brushed the side of her hand against the edge of a tile and gave herself a little cut. Our crew was right on top of it with the first-aid kit. It was this little tiny cut, but from the way our crew reacted—crowding around her, pulling out every available item from the kit, acting like we were in an episode of ER—you'd think she chopped off her whole hand.

3:37 p.m.

We have a visitor on set: Spirit, the dog from next door, has decided to squeeze her head under the fence so she can catch a glimpse of the action. Really I think she's just another girl trying to sneak a peek at Ty. Yet another "rabid" fan.

*June 21st, 2002
Day 2

12:35 p.m.
The funniest thing just happened with Ty and Scott. They were
putting the original wood trim back up in the room, when our
prankster cameraman, Rob, whispered into Scott's ear, "Put caulk
on Ty." Little did Rob know our mild-mannered homeowner would
actually do it! Without missing a beat, Scott used his caulk gun
to ooze caulk not only on Ty, but also all over Ty's hair! Of
course Ty had to retaliate, so he gave Scott some caulk eyebrows.
Comedy. Everyone held their laughter so they wouldn't bust the
shot (that's what we call it when you can hear the crew in the
background and the shot can't be used). But eventually they
couldn't hold it in any longer. They completely cracked up. It was
the kind of funny that makes you cry. The rest of the day was
filled with "caulk head" jokes. Nice.

7:50 p.m.
My mom and stepdad arrived for a visit today. They will be
here through the next episode. We should have fun.

*June 22nd, 2002
Day Off

Good news! My husband found out The Lion King cast will not
be rehearsing for as many days as originally planned when they
move from Denver to Houston. This means he can come visit me
between cities. We'll spend my day off together in Manhattan,
and then he'll be with me for the next episode on Long Island.

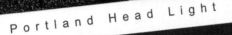

Portland Head Light

* **June 23rd, 2002**
Day 0

We tried to shoot the Open this morning, but it was a complete bust. The fog obliterated the view of Portland Head Light. We couldn't see the lighthouse, the head light, or even the ocean! I guess that's why lighthouses exist, huh? Because Portland Head Light is pretty far from the location of the episode, we were afraid we wouldn't have the chance to come back. Maybe we got a little desperate, because the next thing I knew I was holding up a postcard to the camera exclaiming, "This is what you'd be seeing right now if it weren't so foggy!" Hey, it seemed funny at the time. Well, I think it's kind of funny.

*June 24th, 2002

Day 1: Gorham, Maine
Designers: Laurie & Frank
Neighbors: Laurie & Nicole and Angelica & Ed

Found out this morning that Frank was stuck in the hotel
elevator last night for two hours. That is my nightmare.
Apparently the woman trapped in there with her son felt the
same way. And her nightmare became Frank's nightmare. But if I
know Frank, he probably invited her to dinner at his home in
Texas. Frank has never met a stranger. I can't believe all of
that happened to him in the hotel before I even saw him. He
didn't waste any time adding excitement to Season Three.

*June 25th, 2002

Day 2

9:36 a.m.

I kicked off this morning with quite a dramatic scene.
Unfortunately, it wasn't one for the show. I ran to grab my Paige
Cam, and as I headed back, my ankle gave out on me. I severely
sprained it about 11 years ago, and even after extensive physical
therapy it has never been the same. I've had to be very careful;
it would only take one more severe turn to end my dance career. I
can't explain the despair I would feel if I couldn't dance
anymore.

When my ankle turned over this morning I heard a "snap" and
felt a burn. I immediately jumped to the conclusion that it was
seriously damaged and started crying and calling out for my
mom, who came running over. After I calmed down, I realized that
I hadn't damaged it as much as I thought. I could move it and
walk on it, but I was still concerned about the future of my

We did get back to Portland Head Light today to shoot the open again. It was breathtaking! Definitely worth going back for the shot. Although I secretly wish the editor would choose the foggy shot with the postcard. I still think that's funny.

© Marc Jeff Schirmer

Courtesy of The Museum at Portland Head Light

dancing, so I was pretty down. Frank tried to comfort me by bringing up the possibility of surgery. A doctor had said that with surgery I would lose the flexibility and range of motion I need as a dancer. That's why I didn't go that route before. "When was that?" Frank asked me. "Eleven years ago." He said, "I think there's been some medical advancement since then, dear." It's funny, but I honestly had never thought about that. Frank really helped me see the light at the end of the tunnel.

Drama over. Everyone back to work. I've got to get into makeup and be a host, for goodness' sake!

10:15 a.m.

One nice thing about hurting myself: Everyone is bending over backward to help and to keep me off my feet. My mom just brought pancakes from catering. The caterer put bananas in them just for me. Everyone is bringing me water, asking if I need anything, checking up on me. Not a bad consolation prize. Our crew is the best!!

＊June 26th, 2002

Travel Day *Heading to NYC. Patrick will be there waiting for me. I can't wait to see him.*

＊June 27th, 2002
Day 0

Went to a lake to film the Open and Designer B-roll *(the footage that runs while I introduce the show in a voice-over)* for this episode. It was a riot watching Ty goof off with Frank and our new designer, Edward Walker, for the cameras. At one point, Ty leaped through the air, jumping over their rowboat and into the lake. He is fearless. I was scared just dangling my feet in the water because I didn't know what animal might come up and bite my toes.

✱ June 28th, 2002

Day 1: Long Island, New York
Designers: Frank & Edward
Neighbors: Maria & Brian and Anna & Sal

This is Edward's first shoot. It'll be easy to work with him because we already have such good rapport. Edward was one of our sewing coordinators last season and he was always one of my favorite people to be around. I was so happy for him when he told me that he landed one of the new designer positions. He worked hard for it.

4:32 p.m.

Maria and Brian heard I was writing this book and said to me, *"Write that we're the best homeowners you've ever had."* Well, Brian hurt his back when they were unloading the room and Maria needed a bandage before 9:30 a.m. You're not off to a stellar start, guys.

An iguana's tail cut my lip today. How many people can say that happens when they're at work? Let me explain.

Iggy's television debut!

17

Sal and Anna have a pet iguana named Iggy. I couldn't resist carrying him along when I went to check on Edward and his team. Iggy was being so calm and sweet. But when I entered the room, Maria and Brian cheered and applauded for him, and the noise scared him and he started whippin' around. That tail is like a razor, and it sliced my lip. Whoa! He quieted down after a moment, and I put him back in his cage. Maria told me he loves blueberries, so I gave him some from catering. I made a friend. *(I guess love can hurt, especially when it whips you in the kisser.)*

6:50 p.m.

Ty managed to add a little extra excitement to this challenge: He accidentally spilled an entire can of Frank's color-matched stain all over the driveway! We all gasped. I captured the entire incident on Paige Cam, but I don't know if it will make the final edit of the episode because it happened after "homework" had been assigned. Because of the show's format, it might be difficult to fit in the footage before going to Day 2. It's sad to think no one in America will see it. Yes, it was a tragic error for Frank's room *(he needed that stain!)*, but it was hilarious. Ty tried to save some of the stain by scooping it up with putty spatulas. Again, tragic but hilarious.

* June 29th, 2002
Day 2

4:05 p.m.

The situation in Edward's room went from tense to grim. The consensus is that the armoire that Ty made is never going to fit through the bedroom door. Big problem. They'll have to take off the doors of the armoire if there's even going to be a chance of getting it into the room. That means the doors will have to be adjusted and balanced again. Bigger problem: Ty and the prop master, Eddie, have already left and are on their way to the airport. Our location coordinator, Patrick, will have to take care of this for Ty. Yet another hat Patrick will don in order to move things along.

You know, we've had issues like this before, when everyone says it's bleak. But our crew and our designers always come through. I'm not sure if I should start to worry or not. I fear our hubris may catch up with us someday.

*July 7th, 2002

Day 1: Syossett, New York
Designers: Genevieve & Doug
Neighbors: Carrie & James and
Susan & Robert

Susan is the decorating editor for Good Housekeeping magazine, and boy, can you tell that from her house. It is really beautiful. A part of me wonders why we are even here. She clearly has a knack for decorating. But then again, maybe we can give her some ideas that she would never think of on her own. Really, that's the whole point of our show. Her kitchen definitely needs an update. If there is one room we can help, it's that one! And Genevieve is great with kitchens.

I always set up my makeup mirror and stuff in an extra room in one of the houses. This time I get to use Susan and Robert's master bedroom. It's so lovely in there, and they've been very accommodating. Sometimes it can feel awkward going into the neighbors' houses. I mean, we really take over their world, not just the room that's being redecorated. The participants give up so much control when they're on Trading Spaces. They have to let go of the expectations they have for their own room, they have to let go of doing things their way and of seeing their house as a home. To some degree, their houses become TV sets. We lay runners on the floor, we keep up with the trash, and we're careful, but there is only so much you can do when every room is filled with TV equipment or catering or makeup or supplies, not to mention 20 to 30 people running in and out. And let's not forget the table saws, hammers, compressors, and the construction madness going on outside.

11:59 a.m.

These rooms need lots of demolition work. There's vinyl flooring in Vern's kitchen and wallpaper in Gen's kitchen. Neither is coming up easily, and both rooms are falling behind. Sometimes we luck out and come across wallpaper and flooring that can be removed quickly, but more often than not it's a nightmare.

In the meantime, Vern has put Susan and me to work assembling the buffet hutch. Why does it seem these things are so easy for other people? A couple of production assistants keep offering to help, but I'm shooing them away. I'm on a mission to figure out this crazy hutch, even if it kills me—and in this heat it just might.

6:30 p.m.

The chance that anyone on our two teams will get a decent night's sleep is pretty slim. There's just too much catching up to do, thanks to the huge amount of demolition work in the rooms. Vern will definitely stick around tonight. If I know him, he'll stay until everything from Day 1 is complete. The good news is, as always, if they catch up tonight they'll be on schedule tomorrow. They will be exhausted, but on time.

Gen with Carrie.

Sukanya Krishnan brought out the best in us in her interviews. She's a big fan of <u>Trading Spaces</u> so she really "gets it."

Our teams did stay awake into the wee hours of the morning. I'm impressed. It always moves me when homeowners show that level of commitment to the process. It was either that or they were shamed into it because Vern never left. I swear the only reason he continues to function is caffeine. He is addicted to Diet Coke and can't get enough. Never, ever take the last Diet Coke on set. Vern is a perfect gentleman, but he will just plain hunt you down if you mess with his stash.

11:30 a.m.

A bit of trivia for ya: Theodore Roosevelt was the only U.S. president from Long Island, New York. His home is a few minutes from here, so we shot the Open there. It was an incredible house, made even more remarkable by its grounds. The whole area is a national park site. I wish we could have taken a tour inside the house, but duty called. The park rangers were very gracious and gave us free rein to use the house and gardens. It was one of my favorite Opens ever. It ranked right up there with the Opens we did at Loveland Ski Resort last season.

12:15 p.m.

Susan and Robert own a beautiful pot rack that Genevieve wants to put back up in their kitchen. The problem is that Susan and Robert hid it so we couldn't find it. Clearly, they've learned from watching our show. I always say if you don't want us to touch something in your house, you'd better move it to the next state! Unfortunately for us, even though Genevieve had no intention of painting or altering it, we couldn't find the pot rack. I set out on a mission with Carrie and the Paige Cam to track it down. Then I learned that our location coordinator, Cyndi, had already asked Susan and Robert where the darn thing was. I was bummed that my scavenger hunt was thwarted. So Cyndi said to me jokingly, *"I could hide it again for you."* And I replied, *"OK, would you?!"* So she did! What a riot! She hid that thing well too. The search took forever. Carrie gave up helping me *(which was just as well, because she really needed to be working in the kitchen)*, but eventually I located it. How rewarding. A complete waste of time, but somehow remarkably satisfying.

* July 10th, 2002
Day 0

We shot some summer promotional material for the show. Laird from the on-air promotions team came out to our location with gobs of summer sundries. She brought a grill, towels, bubbles, and all kinds of fun things. At one point she had Amy Wynn, Genevieve, Doug, and me sit at a picnic table in the backyard. I don't know if the bench was simply old or if it was because we moved it to get it out of the sun, but the bench that Amy Wynn and I were sitting on completely collapsed. We screamed in surprise. It was like having the rug pulled out from under us. It was hilarious. I hope it makes it into the promo. Hey, it's good TV.

Eddie, our props master, found himself in quite a pickle when he arrived on location with the pickup truck and trailer. The driveway at one of the houses was way too small to hold the entire Carpentry World setup *(that's what we call the area where the carpenters work)*, and the driveway at the other house sat at the top of an extremely steep hill. Eddie realized that he was in a real bind when he tried to drive up the hill. For starters, the

A moment from the promo shoot

truck could barely even climb to the top. The weight of the trailer actually pulled the truck backward. To make matters worse, the bottom of the hill ended at the ridge of a cliff! Just when we thought he'd made it and everything was OK, Eddie realized that he'd blocked in the pickup truck behind the trailer. No good. We use that truck during the shoots to run out and get supplies. Eddie then had to back the truck and trailer all the way down the hill *(which of course meant blindly heading toward the cliff)*, turn around, and go up the hill in reverse! While he was performing this feat of heroism, the rest of the crew was scrambling to find a willing homeowner in the neighborhood to accommodate our parking needs. But we should have never doubted Eddie for a second. He pulled it off. Astonishing!

We weren't able to shoot the Open today as planned because the truck/trailer incident took a big bite out of our time, but we did finish in time to go out for dinner together. One of the homeowners gave us directions to the little downtown of Katonah, but dinner in the quaint town was not to be. We got lost. In a caravan, we all got lost, driving around aimlessly for an hour. This group slays me. With our level of genius, it's a wonder we ever actually get two rooms done. We gave up and headed to Outback Steakhouse. At least we knew how to get there. Our cameraman, Mark, picked up the check. *What a doll!*

★ July 11th, 2002

Day 1: Katonah, New York
Designers: Genevieve & Doug
Neighbors: Amy & Phil and Amy & Brian

This is a bit of a hoity-toity neighborhood. Apparently lots of celebrities live around here. John Schneider, from The Dukes of Hazard, grew up in Amy and Brian's house. Cool. One of Martha Stewart's many homes is nearby. And Chevy Chase's. The community is very protective of this area, and town ordinance requires that a police officer be present at all times during the taping of the show. So this Matt fella is gonna be around for the next two days. He's super-nice and even helped unload Amy and Brian's room!

12:45 p.m.

Amy Wynn gave me a great shirt to wear for this episode. It's a black tank top with a strip of hook-and-loop tape across the front. It comes with letters you can use to spell words on the shirt. The makeup artist and I are having a blast thinking up clever words to put on the shirt, depending on what's happening in the rooms. We've also been thinking of ways we could use the shirt to trick the homeowners or throw them off. I suggested wearing "THE ISSUE" and pretending I forgot to change the

Day 2

For two long days we had been discussing the delicate situation of the wood floors being so old and soft. They were exquisite, but very difficult to work around. The team wanted to fix them with a floor sander, but Amy Wynn and Eddie refused, saying the machine was too powerful and would make the floors uneven. The disagreement even created some tension between Wynn and the team. Dealing with the floors was a real nightmare, and suffice it to say, they weighed very heavily on our minds the entire time.

Even with the pressure of time, we paused for some R+R.

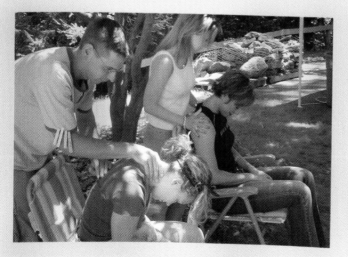

letters before switching houses. Imagine the poor homeowners panicking over some phantom "issue" they thought might be happening at their place. Hee hee. I feel so devilish.

* July 12th, 2002
Day 2

11:32 a.m.
Well, I tried wearing "THE ISSUE" across my shirt. It didn't work. The homeowners were too busy to even notice. Bummer.

4:57 p.m.
We used Matt, the police officer, to our advantage. Our producer, Natalie, came up with a funny idea for a shot to run in the credits of the episode. She had Matt pretend to arrest me. I cried out, *"I swear, we were on time and on budget! Don't arrest me!"* Matt, as serious as could be, handcuffed me and pushed me into his cop car. My shirt read "BUSTED." He did a great job—didn't break character at all. I even started to believe him!

We had a bit of a scare in Amy and Brian's house at the end of the day. We had just wrapped the Designer Chats *(when I interview each designer about the finished room)* and were getting ready for the pièce de résistance: the Reveals. In the meantime, the production assistants put away all the supplies and tools, including the protective runners for the floors and stairs. Suddenly we heard the crashing sound of something falling down the steps. Everyone gasped, thinking Gary, our PA, had fallen. Fearfully, we peered around the corner and saw that it was only the portable vacuum. With concerns of Gary's broken bones set aside, our minds immediately went to the same thought—the floors! We checked the stairs in silence. They looked good. We sighed in relief and went back to work. Later I learned that Amy did see a slight nick. I'm still glad it wasn't Gary who fell.

Amy and Brian loved their room. And Genevieve used the antique ice tongs I bought for her back in Maine. Yeah!! I knew she'd find a place for them someday.

*July 14th, 2002
Day 0

Found a Container Store! Oh, I've needed to come across one of those. The cardboard boxes that hold my Trading Spaces wardrobe have been a shameful mess for months. They are all ripped and barely hanging together. Because my wardrobe travels in the truck, Eddie has been asking me to get suitcases or something, but I knew there had to be a better way. I'm an organization freak and I LOVE The Container Store. However, the best method of organizing my wardrobe for personal convenience and storage in the truck was eluding me. I stood transfixed by all the options, unable to make any choices. I even brought all my torn boxes inside the store, hoping it would help me eye what I needed. I was a sad and comical sight.

Thankfully, a sales associate rescued me. Leave it to the experts. Larissa had the best ideas. In no time she whipped up the perfect set of bins and bags. My shabby, embarrassing boxes of clothes turned into a tidy, easily transportable wardrobe: One bin for jackets and coats, one for boots and belts, one for sandals and shoes, and one for pants and shirts. Unfortunately, some of the items I needed weren't in stock, but Larissa said the store expected a shipment the next day. She offered to drive the stuff out to me on location and help switch my wardrobe over to the new containers. How sweet is that?! I asked if she was sure she wanted to do such a long drive since the location was about an hour away. She said, *"Are you kidding me?!! I'd love to come."* It wasn't entirely selfless. She was dying to meet the designers and visit the set. Cool. So I guess I'll see her tomorrow.

* July 15th, 2002

Day 1: Monroe, New York
Designers: Frank & Kia
Neighbors: Randi & Kim and Dawn & Matt

Because the shoot is so far away, I was up at 4:30 a.m. to work out. I'm in the habit of working out in the mornings, because even when I get back to the hotel at a decent hour at night I can't bring myself to go to the fitness room. I just crash. Somehow, it's the lesser of two evils for me to get up early and know that I'm done. But 4:30 a.m. may be pushing it, even for me.

* July 18th, 2002

Day Off

This was one of the most suspenseful days of my year so far: This morning the Prime Time Emmy nominations were announced. I wanted so badly for our show to be recognized—it would mean so much to us and to Denise Cramsey, our executive producer. She's put her heart and soul into this show.

At the beginning of the week, E! Television had let me know they wanted me standing by via phone on the morning of the nominations so they could call me if Trading Spaces was named. I thought that would be so cool. Then I found out they announce the nominations at 6:00 a.m. Los Angeles time. That meant 7:00 a.m. for me and my husband in Houston *(that's where he is now with The Lion King tour).* That's pretty early for Patrick because he gets home so late from the theatre. No matter though. We waited

July 15th, 3:30 p.m.

Larissa showed up with my gear. And better yet, she came with presents for the entire cast. She helped me reorganize everything, which was extremely kind, considering it was excruciatingly hot and humid outside. There we were, two sweaty gals, surrounded by piles of old boxes and stacks of new bins. But when we were done, the backseat of the truck was a vision of organization.

by the phone in anticipation of the announcement.

After a lot of hoopla and interviews and predictions on E!, the moment came. Laura Innes and Eric McCormack took the podium and read the nominations for several categories, none of which were ours. After the big announcement, nominations from additional categories scrolled across the bottom of the screen. Where was our category!! Come to think of it, what **was** our category?!! I watched The Osbournes come up. Wouldn't that be our category? The phone wasn't ringing. I called Denise on my cell. She was up early too, waiting in anticipation, and was running her husband ragged, frantically dictating to him what websites to try. She eventually had to give up and leave for work. When I spoke to her, she sounded pretty disappointed. I suggested she try to reach the TLC publicist and get her to find out one way or the other. But before Denise even heard back from the publicist, she called me to say, "Paige, I think we got it. I think we got it. I just got a call from a friend, congratulating me. That must be what she's talking about. Oh my God. I'll call you back when I know for sure."

Well, at this point all I know for sure is E! didn't call and my husband desperately wants to go back to sleep. He's begging me to come to bed. But I can't. I'm too wound up and excited. Then Denise calls back, *"Congratulations! We are nominated for Outstanding Special Class Program!"* Her name is on the ballot, as are mine and Stephen Schwartz's, executive producer from TLC, and the field producers'. The award will be handed out at the pre-ceremony on September 14 in Pasadena, one week before the televised Prime Time Emmys.

Our competition is:
- *AFI's 100 Years...100 Thrills, America's Most Heart-Pounding Movies (CBS)*
- *I Love Lucy 50th Anniversary Special (CBS)*
- *Survivor (CBS)*
- *The West Wing: Documentary Special (NBC)*

We are the only cable show in our category. We're competing with the big guns now! This is truly thrilling. In the words of Frank Bielec, "Not bad for a pissant cable show."

* July 21st, 2002

Day 1: Rockville Centre, New York
Designers: Edward & Vern
Neighbors: Jinnette & Ken and Tara & Miles

10:00 a.m.

The neighbors came out to the street to do the Key Swap and I immediately noticed that three of them had cut off the sleeves of their Trading Spaces shirts. Participants do this sometimes and it's pretty cool, but this year we have the logos of our sponsors on the sleeves. Lowe's has been on the shirts for a few episodes already, and today our newest sponsor, Swiffer, appeared on the shirts for the first time. Cutting off the sleeves wouldn't be the worst thing ever, and we can stop it from happening again, but the Swiffer "people" are visiting the set today. Oops. Oh well, too late.

The neighbors are a riot! Ken is so funny. And they're all really good at the TV thing. We often shoot the Key Swap a few times because of sound or tape problems. These guys are so good at making it like the first time for each take. Ken keeps surprising me—he's very spontaneous. Love that!

*July 22nd, 2002
Day 2

Once again, Vern stayed until the wee hours of the morning. Ken kept up with him from project to project through the night. Neither of them was giving up before they finished hanging the train track above the bed. (*Vern's theme was "planes, trains, and automobiles."*) I think they really bonded, because this morning I heard them telling stories about their overnight efforts, and one of them actually used the phrase, *"I love you, man."*

3:52 p.m.

All is not lovey-dovey at Edward's house. Major fabric fiasco! Apparently the silk fabric for the wall behind the bed was in a black plastic bag, hidden from eyesight of the other team and safe from any blunders. Little did we know, it would become a blunder of its own. Edward was looking all over for the silk when he suddenly realized what must have happened. When cleaning up the room, someone mistook the bag with the fabric for an actual trash bag and threw all the used paint trays and brushes into it. **Aaaaaaargh!!!**

Edward was frozen in his tracks for just one horrifying moment and

then he dove for the "trash bag" with such a flurry that he was almost a blur. He whipped the bag over, dumping everything out— paint trays, brushes, and all. Sure enough, there was the dark green silk, completely covered in light green paint. To top it off, paint now splattered the carpet too, because some of it seeped off the plastic runner when Edward overturned the bag. Everyone was quiet. Edward was completely still. Expletives were poised on his lips, but he walked away in absolute silence with only a barely audible grunt. The rest of us stood in shock, not knowing what to do. How do you get paint out of silk? It was almost 4:00 p.m. on Day 2! There was no more time, or money for that matter. It seemed dismal.

Our associate producer, Mindy, checked on Edward. He was at the end of the block, smoking like a chimney as he tried to hold on to his composure. I know he was afraid he was going to explode. Mindy came back to the house and told us Edward wanted the fabric laid out flat so he could assess the damage. She wanted to start trying to get the paint out of the fabric. I said, "Look, if Edward wants us to lay it out, then that's exactly what we're going to do, and nothing else." With vigorous determination, I grabbed a tarp for the living room and directed everyone to help me spread the silk out on the floor.

We waited for Edward to come back into the house. You could cut the tension with a knife. He entered as silently as he had left. With cigarette still in hand (no care that he was now smoking without apology in the home of one of our participants), he stood over the fabric, stoically inspecting the damaged areas of the silk. He stared at the fabric, took a drag from his cigarette, stared at the fabric some more, and then, without explanation, he called out for a tape measure. The call went out: "A tape measure. Edward needs a tape measure. Get a tape measure." We couldn't imagine what he wanted to measure, or why,

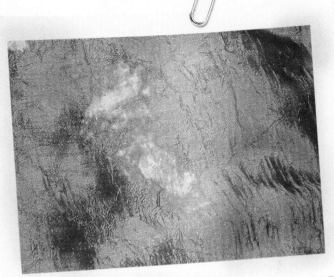

Paint on silk is no laughing matter...

A rare moment: Edward caught without a smile.

but it soon became clear. He had noticed that almost all the paint was on one end of the fabric. The bed would hide any fabric that was 28 inches or below. We held our breath as he measured how high up the paint had landed on the fabric. Now you're going to think I'm exaggerating, but I swear he measured exactly 28 inches! We stood in amazement, and then in a gush of relief, started laughing and celebrating. The color came back in Edward's cheeks, and we prepared to finish the room. I think that was about as close to a miracle as any of us on Trading Spaces had ever seen. We were so happy. Cheers all around, except from our poor location coordinator who was left with the task of getting the paint out of the carpet. Sorry, Patrick.

* July 24th, 2002
Day 0

I'm doing my first round of voice-overs for Season Three today. I'm really looking forward to it. This is one of my favorite parts of the job. Whenever a few episodes reach the final edit stage, I go into a studio and record the voice-overs. Denise calls in and the audio engineer patches her through so we can hear each other. She directs me during the session and we have a great time. And we look for any excuse to talk. If the audio engineer is changing tape or breaks for any reason, that's license to gab in my book. This time Denise will be in the studio with me because we're taping shows in Philadelphia, where Banyan Productions is based. My Aunt Eileen and Uncle Joel, who live in Philly, are coming with me. It'll be a little voice-over party.

1:35 p.m.
We're headed out to the location for the next episode. I've gotta get into makeup and get dressed for the Open. My outfit

36

this time is a Trading Spaces first: I'm wearing a skirt! Our producer, Larry, convinced me to do it. He planned to shoot me on a golf driving range, so I shopped like a fiend the other day

Jerod, my patient golf instructor

3:30 p.m.

We're at the driving range, which is a multiplex of fun. Larry will shoot the B-roll here: The designers will play miniature golf and the neighbors will race go-carts and hit balls in the batting cage. Me? I'm supposed to do this golf thing. It's a hilarious joke, though, because I do not have the slightest idea how to golf. I asked around to see if someone here could give me a quick lesson (preferably someone really cute). They introduced me to Jerod, and he is indeed a cutie-pitutie. I'm not sure the lesson will do me any good, but maybe it will keep me from looking like a complete idiot.

5:00 p.m.

Can't say that I managed to hit many balls with flair. Can't really say I managed to hit many balls, period. But I gave it the ol' college try, and Jerod pretended to be proud, which was sweet.

Denise has invited all of us to her home for a barbecue. So many crew members live in Philly that it's almost like a reunion.

trying to find something that would work as a golfing skirt. Tommy Hilfiger to the rescue! The skirt is cute, sassy, and sexy. Love it. I hope I love it as much when I see myself on camera.

* July 25th, 2002

Day 1: Montgomeryville, Pennsylvania
Designers: Kia & Doug
Neighbors: Marissa & Dave and Suzi & Wendy

The mayor came by with a cake for the cast and crew. What a welcoming gesture!

* July 26th, 2002

Day 2

Marissa and Dave are exhausted. It is extremely hot in the attic room they're decorating, and it looks like they're about to drop. The heat may be affecting them in other ways too. They are getting very sentimental. I asked Dave if he was still having a good time in spite of the heat. He got very serious and said he wouldn't trade this experience for anything. He loved our crew and felt that we worked like a family. Then he got a little teary-eyed and said, "I feel like I'm a part of that family now."

* July 30th, 2002

Day 1: Shamong, New Jersey
Designers: Frank & Doug
Neighbors: Peggy & Rick and Christie & Michael

This location is over an hour away from where we're staying. That means another early-morning workout. Being far from the location can take its toll. I decided not to drive my own car and carpooled with the two producers, Larry and Aimee. Much better.

It is unbearably hot and humid today. There is quite a respite in Peggy and Rick's house because their air-conditioning rocks! But in Christie and Michael's house, it's another story. I can hardly tell if their air-conditioning is even on. And Frank is working in that house. I'm afraid he'll drop from a heart attack. He can't stand the heat.

Here's where all the furniture from the living room landed!! Forget cooking supper, it's take-out tonight.

4:42 p.m.

Doug's team made a group decision not to paint all the way through the kitchen, even though that means the ceiling will only be half painted. Christie and Michael felt strongly about it. Since it would be almost impossible to complete so large a task in the two-day time frame, they felt it would be more productive to put their energies toward the room itself and worry about the kitchen another time. I think it was a wise choice, because at the moment the kitchen is completely cluttered and crammed with the old furniture from the room. The team would have to unload the entire kitchen just to begin on the ceiling. Our viewers might not think about (*or if they do, they never find out about*) what happens to the stuff that's loaded out of the room before the team begins redecorating. Well, it gets put other places in the house, wherever it can fit. This time it was in the kitchen. Believe me, to move it at this point would be a terrible headache. Christie and Michael say they'll help Peggy and Rick move the furniture and finish painting the ceiling after we leave.

Day 1: Philadelphia, Pennsylvania
Designers: Genevieve & Edward
Neighbors: Amy & Rich and Patti & Chris

This will be a fun shoot for me. We're in the middle of downtown Philadelphia, and I have great memories here. We're shooting right in the inner city bustle, so there will be lots of logistical problems to take into account. But many of our headaches have already been solved with the help of The Franklin Institute, a wonderful science museum. Shooting in an urban location involves finding parking, obtaining permits, determining where Carpentry World will fit, etc. The Franklin Institute offered us free parking in their covered lot and allowed us to set up Carpentry World on their back lot. They've also given us permission to shoot inside their building. Our producer, Natalie, wants to shoot the Open, Time's Up, and Designer B-roll in there. Awesome. The Franklin Institute is very special to me. I used to beg my Aunt Eileen and Uncle Joel to take me there whenever I came to Philly to visit. So I'm especially excited to tape some of the show there.

* *August 7th, 2002*

Day 2

11:30 a.m.

We met Evan and Emily, PR folks for The Franklin Institute, in the lobby of the museum. They seemed as excited to have us there as I was to be there. They showed us around and helped facilitate all our needs. We shot the Time's Up in the electricity exhibit. I said, "Don't be shocked, but time's up." Oh, will the

40

comedy ever end? Then we took some bumper footage (what we use right before and after commercial breaks). I asked Evan if they had access to a stethoscope in the museum. I wanted to pretend to be listening to the Heart, which is an enormous model of the human heart located in the museum. It is so big that you can actually climb through it. I loved playing in it as a kid. The path takes you through the chambers of the heart, from auricle to auricle, ventricle to ventricle. You pass the pulmonary artery and the aorta while hearing the rumble of a heartbeat. There are usually a dozen or more kids playing in and around the Heart. It's practically a Philadelphia institution.

After the Heart shot, Evan and Emily took us to the pendulum. As a child, I stared down the spiral

Photo courtesy of The Franklin Institute

staircase surrounding the pendulum, wanting to go to the bottom and look at the motion up close. But when I would get three floors away from the bottom I would be stopped by a "Staff Only" sign. Well, today that sign

At the Franklin
Institute...
the gravity of the
situation was very
moving. (hee hee)

should have read "Paige Davis and Staff Only" because we walked right past it and over the rope. The pendulum was stunning. The sand glistened and the intricate marble was beautiful. It amazed me how such a large, overwhelming apparatus could move in such a delicate way. I never realized just how precise it was until I saw it up close. It seems obvious that precision would be of utmost importance for a timepiece, but I still found it fascinating to watch the enormous, heavy metal bulb glide past a little three-inch peg without knocking it down, until the one precise moment that marked that time of day. I wanted to shoot the Time's Up at the pendulum, but the crew said it was too difficult to get enough of the pendulum in camera range. So we did a funny bump shot utilizing the pendulum instead. I hope it makes it into the final edit.

August 8th, 2002
Day Off

I didn't plan to go to NYC today, but I'm on my way. A couple of days ago, Lifestyles magazine called to tell me that all the pictures they took for the cover were ruined. Something actually happened to the film. So I'm off to do a reshoot. It is very fortunate that we are shooting Trading Spaces in Philadelphia right now, because it's so easy to get up to NYC from here.

3:25 p.m.

Famous last words. I was stuck in traffic for over three hours. (It's only supposed to take an hour and a half to get there.) I thought I might pull my hair out, but I'm glad I went. I had a wonderful time with Gideon Lewin, the photographer. He brings out the best in me. For this reshoot I wore my own clothes instead of what their stylist brought the first time around. I was so much more comfortable. I know the shots will come out great, maybe even sexy. Ooh la la.

8:35 p.m.

Being in New York means I can take a dance class again. The folks in class told me they'd seen the "Trading Places" wardrobe-trade spread I did with Jane Clayson in People magazine. It's four pages, which is cool. The first two pages show fun shots of the two of us in our swapped attire—I'm in an ever-so-news-anchor gray pantsuit; Jane has on an ever-so-Trading Spaces pair of jeans and leather jacket. The third page has our interviews and comments. On the fourth page, we are "switched back" and wearing our own wardrobes. It's weird looking at myself. I can't figure out what I think about it. None of my friends seem to have a problem expressing their thoughts on the subject. It's kind of funny. Such intense opinions. Some LOVE it. Others say the suit is unfortunate, and I'm prettier in person. There's just no pleasing everyone. I don't really care. It's a four-page spread in People, for Pete's sake. I'm just glad it's in there. What a neat thing.

* August 9th, 2002
Day 0

I have a fun event scheduled for this morning. Emily and Evan from The Franklin Institute asked me if I'd like to participate in the Institute's Xtravaganza Weekend celebrating the upcoming summer 2002 X Games. I'm excited to do an event sponsored by The Franklin Institute. I love that place so much. To kick off the celebration, K'NEX toys will construct a giant record-setting mural of a skateboarder soaring over the Philadelphia skyline. The mural will include a total of 183,456 plastic K'NEX pieces, consisting of 61,152 connectors and 122,304 rods. The resulting image will stand 26 feet wide and over 36 feet high. They've asked me to put on the ceremonial first piece. Cool.

2:45 p.m.
It was fun meeting all the kids who came out to work on the mural. We had lots of photo ops, and the staff tried to give as many kids as possible the chance to be in a picture. Some of the photos will end up in the newspaper—the kids were thrilled. One little girl whispered in my ear very timidly, "I've never been in the paper before." I could tell from her voice that this was one of the most exciting things to ever happen to her.

I can remember how awed I felt the very first time my name appeared in the paper. I had won a reading contest at the local

5762 lifestyles
30TH YEAR

international edition · united states · canada

www.lifestylesmagazine.com

2002 · vol. 30 · no. 181 · $7.00

a lifestyles exclusive:

Paige Davis
Building A Career

in this issue:

library in Sun Prairie, Wisconsin. I looked at my picture for
hours and read my name over and over. I felt singled out. I felt
special. Of course, they spelled my name wrong. When I was a
kid, whenever I was in the paper I was either "Mendy," "Mandy," or
"Mindi." (Mindy is my first name. I use my middle name, Paige, as
my stage name.) I don't know what was so hard about Mindy, but it
never failed. Even early on I was learning the rough truths
about the media.

* August 10th, 2002

Day 1: Newtown, Pennsylvania
Designers: Frank & Vern
Neighbors: Vicki & Rourke and Barb & James

Today has been so much fun. Because Banyan Productions is
located in Philadelphia, almost all the crew lives here. So we
have had an onslaught of family and friends visiting the set to
check out the hit show their loved ones have been working on for
the past year. My sister, Brooke, and her boyfriend, Lu, even
came for a visit and they live in Pittsburgh! Of course, Aunt
Eileen and Uncle Joel hung out too. It was touching to meet
everyone's parents and family. I worked with these guys all last
season, but somehow it feels like I know them even better after
meeting their families.

2:57 p.m.

Brooke and Lu really jumped in and helped. In Frank's room,
they helped take the hinges off the cabinets, and they primed,
painted, and rehung the cabinet doors. Lu even sewed shut all
the pillows in Vern's room. Nothing, not even the heat, deterred
them from pitching in. Now that's the kind of visitors we like on
the set. I was so proud. Hopefully my sister will fly out to

Phoenix later in the season to visit me and become an official
production assistant for those episodes. Then she can actually
get paid for all that hard work.

8:00 p.m.

I had dinner with Brooke and Lu back at Aunt Eileen and
Uncle Joel's. It's been a wonderful day.

* August 11th, 2002
Day 2

We shot the Open at a covered bridge. *Beautiful.*

Vern stayed up all night to make sure his carpentry project
was completed. It was a huge cabinet that ran the entire length
of the room and was designed to hold all of the family's media
equipment. He's been told not to pull all-nighters anymore, but
sometimes you just can't change a person's habits. I hope he
makes it through the rest of the day. And I hope his homeowners
can hang in there too. They stayed up with him and right now
they all look pretty haggard.

7:30 p.m.

Something came over me when I revealed Barb and James's room
to them. Maybe it was because I knew they had worked so hard
all night, or maybe I was just tired, but when Barb opened her
eyes and started to cry with joy, I started to cry too. I couldn't
hold back. I was moved to tears. It's incredibly moving to see
what a powerful impact Trading Spaces makes on people's lives.
And knowing that Barb and James had poured absolutely every
ounce of themselves into their neighbors' room made me so happy
to see them happy. I guess I have yet to become immune to those
emotions. I don't really see that ever happening.

* August 12th, 2002
Day 0

More radio interviews.

* August 13th, 2002
Day 1: Collegeville, Pennsylvania
Designers: Frank & Doug
Neighbors: Lynn & Mark and Tish & Tighe

10:42 a.m.

We've hardly begun work on the rooms and I'm already nervous, but this is just like me. Doug has given us cause for concern, though. He's planning a theme room and has hinted that these two days could be "like another Pullman car." *(He's referring to one of his more infamous rooms from last season.)* When he says this, we know he doesn't mean the decor because we already know he's doing a safari theme. He's referring to the amount of work and the possibility of late hours. With Doug, Time's Up doesn't seem to carry much weight.

3:56 p.m.

I tried to do my part to help things go smoothly in Doug's room. I went to Daniel, the sewing coordinator, and asked if I could do anything to help get things ready for the team. He sat me down in front of a serger to prep the bedspread. I'm glad he had such faith in me, but that was probably a mistake. For starters, I think it took him more time to teach me, correct my mistakes, and check my progress than if he had just prepped it himself. Also, I didn't do such a great job. I felt bad. I even apologized to Doug because I didn't want him to think Daniel did that crappy job. Daniel assured me it wasn't as bad as I thought, but he did take out one whole row of stitches to do over. Oops.

8:55 p.m.

Doug definitely has grand
plans for this "Suburban Safari"
bedroom, so a few crew members will stick
around to help the team with their homework—we
sometimes do this if it looks like the team can't get the work
done by morning. We all want this room to be finished in a
timely manner tomorrow. We ordered Chinese food and took a
short break. It was nice. It felt like a big family. Our usual
sibling teasing and ribbing broke out. I think Tish and Tighe
got an earful of our antics, but we had a blast. And I think we
were all glad we stayed.

* August 14th, 2002
Day 2

I've no one to blame but myself, but I can't believe what I
just did! I was Paige-Camming Doug and accidentally brushed

against the dresser he had painted. It was still wet from the red faux finish he's been perfecting on all the bedroom furniture. I can't even remember what the darn Paige Cam was about. Not only did I think I'd ruined my pants, but I was going to have a very difficult time finishing the episode without the other team seeing the red on my pants when I went to the other house.

Doug tells me not to worry; the paint will come out with mineral spirits. That's paint thinner for all you laypeople like me. For some stupid reason I decided to leave my pants on while dousing the paint stain with mineral spirits. I planned on rinsing the spot with water, but got called to the other house to catch something else on Paige Cam. The red stain was definitely out, so I headed over to the other house, completely forgetting about the PAINT THINNER still soaking into my thigh.

All of sudden, I felt this unbearable burning on my leg. I stripped my pants down in one fell swoop. I had actually managed to give myself a chemical burn. Leave it to me. I took my pants all the way off and wrapped up in a towel.

I lay on the sofa, propped my feet up, and put a bag of frozen shrimp on my thigh. *(There wasn't a bag of frozen peas.)* What a sight! To make matters worse, even though the mineral spirits took out the paint stain, it left a huge ring! So now I had to finish the rest of the episode with a big oil mark on my pants. Nice. I think the worst part was how embarrassed I felt for getting myself into that situation in the first place.

Later...

Our producer donated two stuffed gorillas to Doug's room. He hung them from the bamboo grid they installed last night.

Day Off

2:45 a.m.

This turned out to be one of the most fun days of my entire
life. This is the day I picked my dress for the Emmys! My luck
began when I happened to meet a stylist, Leon Hall, in the
airport a few weeks ago. We started talking, and he made a
comment about the success and popularity of Trading Spaces. I
remarked that it was all amazing and wonderful and I mentioned
our Emmy nomination. He asked which designer was dressing me
for the award ceremony. I told him I didn't know, adding that I'd
purchased my own Richard Tyler couture dress for the Daytime
Emmys. He was aghast. "That will never happen again," he said.
He offered immediately to style me, gave me his card, and made
me promise to call him. He said he *"just knew"* that we would
become the best of friends. I was dubious, to say the least. I
mean, what was in it for him? Sure, I'd get the dress lent to me
for free, but how much would the fee be for his services?!
Eventually I threw caution to the wind and just went for it. It
was the best move I ever made. Leon turned out to be one of the
kindest, most generous men I've ever met.

We made plans to meet today. I was still a little nervous
because I didn't know a great deal about the man, other than the
fact that he's a cohost on E! Fashion Emergency and he does
style gossip with Joan and Melissa Rivers after all the award
shows. Leon told me he was taking me to see Carmen Marc Valvo. I
had never heard of Carmen Marc Valvo, but suddenly I was on
pins and needles.

Carmen and his staff pulled some dresses for me to try. One
caught my attention right away. It was a gold two-piece

Bohemian-looking dress—very textured, very hip. I put it on and I loved it. It seemed as though Leon loved it. I didn't want to try on any more. Why? I'd found the dress for me. Carmen and his folks convinced me that I should at least look at the others, if only for fun. Well, that just complicated matters because I fell in love with another dress. Now I had to choose. Carmen didn't seem thrilled with either dress. He liked them (*after all, he did design them*), but he seemed distant, as if he wasn't completely satisfied. From nowhere, he pulled out another dress. I slipped it on, and it was unanimous. THAT was the dress for me. Later we realized why he was so distant. He was contemplating if he should offer me a dress that was brand new to the line and hadn't even premiered on the runway.

* August 21st, 2002

Day 1: Nazareth, Pennsylvania
Designers: Vern & Doug
Neighbors: Christine & Philip and Monique & Mike

Watching Monique trying to figure out how to use a staple gun got me to thinking about another reason people probably watch Trading Spaces: It is empowering. People realize that they don't have to be Bob Vila to make big changes to their homes.

* August 23rd, 2002

Day 0

Doug is going to Brazil soon to judge a design competition. Cool. He asked me to help him tape an interview to be used as a promotional/bio reel that will introduce him to the audience at the awards ceremony.

Photo by Maria Chanadoha Valentino

Carmen
on the
runway

☀ *August 26th, 2002*

Day Off

Today I went to New York City to meet Leon Hall at Fred
Leighton. We chose the jewelry for my Emmy dress. Chandelier
earrings and a bracelet—$75,000 worth of 19th-century
diamonds. **OH MY GOD!**

* August 28th, 2002

Day 1: Manayunk, Pennsylvania
Designers: Frank & Hildi
Neighbors: Karyn & Mary-Frances and Erica & Jen

The soccer episode! These gals are from The Charge, the women's pro soccer team in Philadelphia. They gave me an official jersey to wear on the shoot. It says "DAVIS" on the back and I got to pick my number. I chose number 22, my dad's longtime basketball number. I'm wearing cargo pants instead of jeans. It's like *"Casual Friday for Paige."*

8:15 a.m.

Live shot from location for the local NBC affiliate.

* September 5th, 2002

Day 1: Ashburn, Virginia
Designers: Kia & Hildi
Neighbors: Charisse & Mike and Rachel & Brad

10:00 a.m.

There are so many reporters that we have four PR reps from TLC escorting them around. This is becoming the norm for Season Three. So are the fans gathered in the street. They're trying to catch a glimpse of the action and get autographs and pictures. Sometimes it gets so crazy that fans want pictures and autographs from anyone affiliated with the show in any capacity. Lately even our production assistants, producers, and cameramen get chased down the street. In my opinion, that's how it should be. Those folks work tirelessly to put each show together. I think they get a real kick out of the attention from the fans. It's a little bit of appreciation for our unsung heroes.

12:23 p.m.

Some important TLC executives are on location today. I thought they were here to check things out, see how things work, and get an idea of what it's like out on the road. But they also came to deliver a gift to every person in the cast and crew. To congratulate and thank everyone for the Emmy nomination, they gave us show jackets—just like the ones given to the cast and crew members of Broadway shows! Cool!!! Everyone was really touched. We work so hard and put our hearts and souls into every episode. It meant a great deal to be recognized.

* September 6th, 2002
Day 2

I was sitting with Brad and Rachel after prepping them for the Reveal, when Rachel said that she had an antique tapestry from India that she wanted to give to either Kia or Hildi. It's worth a great deal of money, so I can't understand why she'd want to give it away. She told me it was a gift and she never really appreciated its true value because she dislikes it so much. Since she'll never put it up, she thought maybe one of the designers could use it for a Trading Spaces room or even keep it for themselves.

Well, my stomach began to turn, because at that very moment in Rachel and Brad's house, Kia was adding the final touches of an East Indian decor to their bedroom.

What did Rachel mean?! Did she hate **ALL** Indian stuff?! Kelle, the makeup artist, was sitting near us and heard the whole conversation. I was afraid that if I looked toward Kelle, I'd tip off Rachel and Brad to the design of their room. It took everything in my power to act naturally. But I could feel Kelle's tension behind me and I knew we had to come up with a nonchalant exit so we could explode.

When we got away, we ran straight to Kia's house to warn her and the two producers that Rachel would probably hate her new room. A homeowner's opinion of a Trading Spaces room does not always have to be favorable, but Rachel and Brad went through a rather grueling experience installing a professional rock climbing wall for their friends' son's bedroom. I was quite certain the day would end with them being disappointed in their redecorated bedroom and I just couldn't take it.

When it came time for Rachel and Brad's Reveal, I was so nervous. Charisse and Mike had just seen their son's bedroom, and they **LOVED it!** In fact, I'd say it was one of the most exciting, happy, and overjoyed Reveals I've ever seen on the show. So then I really felt anxious about how Rachel and Brad would react to their bedroom. To be on such a high and know that the crashing low is about to ensue is very alarming.

When it came time to walk them into their room, I kept stalling. I walked extra slowly, and even when we were in place, I rambled on and on. I always get excited before the Reveals, but this time my stomach was doing flip-flops. I wanted the happiness to last just a little longer and I knew the good vibe would end as soon as they saw their East Indian-inspired bedroom.

As I stalled in the bedroom, I could see the producer out of the corner of my eye, motioning me to get on with it. I took a deep breath and told Rachel and Brad to open their eyes. *Wouldn't you know it . . .* they were absolutely thrilled and delighted with the room! I got myself all worked up for nothing. I was in shock, but I was tremendously delighted and relieved!

Rachel still gave her Indian tapestry to Kia, who thought it was fantastic. Even though Rachel never liked the piece, it was a generous and considerate exchange. And because she loved her room so much, she saw giving the tapestry to Kia as a gift, rather than just giving it away.

I tell ya, I'd never have guessed in a million years that this episode would turn out the way it did. When will I learn to stop predicting how the homeowners will react? Frankly, there is no way to predict. I don't know why I let myself go down that road. Usually I am surprised by the reactions and comments I hear from our homeowners. There's no understanding the mysterious ways in which people will deal with change. Life is unpredictable, *and believe me,* so is Trading Spaces.

* September 7th, 2002
Day 0

Today we knocked out the Opens for both upcoming episodes. The first was at the monument commemorating the landing at Iwo Jima. I had been to Washington, D.C., when traveling with the national tour of Beauty and the Beast, but never made it farther than Arlington Cemetery to see this incredible monument. That's one of the perks about having a career that demands a lot of travel—you are always exposed to new surroundings and sights.

Later in the afternoon, I changed wardrobes and did the next Open in front of the Capitol. It was stunning against the blue sky. Washington, D.C., brings out very powerful patriotism in me. I get a little overwhelmed by the grandeur and solemnity of our history and the ever-evolving policies debated and determined inside the walls of almost every building in that city. It kind of blows my mind.

* September 8th, 2002

Day 1: Arlington, Virginia

Designers: Doug & Hildi

Neighbors: Cheryll & Torrey and Elaine & Sean

Dad and Katie visited the set for the first time.

* September 9th, 2002

Day 2

Brad, from the Ashburn episode, showed up on location in Arlington. He said they still love their new East Indian bedroom and only made minor changes to make it more suitable to their everyday needs. I'm so glad they've kept the design. Many times, homeowners appear ecstatic when they see their new rooms, but we find out afterward that they've changed everything. Doug's safari bedroom in Collegeville, PA, is a good example: A few weeks later, the couple sent us a picture of a tiny lizard they found in one of the plants used in their room. *(Crazy—an actual lizard!)* They also sent a photo of their bedroom, completely restored to its pre-Trading Spaces state! They seemed so psyched with it in the Reveal. Weird. Knowing they painted over those zebra stripes just stabs me in the heart because they were so cool and painstaking to complete.

* September 10th, 2002

Day 0

11:00 a.m.

There's no suitable place to set up Carpentry World. The spot they scouted doesn't work because the trailer can't negotiate the narrow driveway. When Eddie tried to drive through, the curbs on either side of the driveway practically ripped off the bottom of the trailer.

1:35 p.m.

Eddie has tried to find a new location for the trailer and all the equipment, but to no avail. He will have to leave it parked in the street next to the original spot.

6:00 p.m.

The crew has wrapped for the day inside the houses. We took the "before" shots and completed the interviews with the homeowners. Unfortunately, we cannot leave until the security guard arrives to watch the trailer. We're told this neighborhood is pretty dangerous, so we can't leave the trailer unprotected. Needless to say, we're all a little concerned about waiting around. Who's gonna guard us?! We figure it's better to wait in a pack.

Gary standing guard...

10:00 p.m.

I left the site a couple of hours ago, but just found out that two of our folks are still waiting for that security guard to arrive. We thought he was supposed to show up by 8:15 p.m. so a few of us took off. Well, Cyndi and Gary are still there, protecting each other and the trailer and wondering what happened to the security guard. Goodness. What a long day for them.

✱ September 11th, 2002

Day 1: NW Washington, D.C.
Designers: Vern & Genevieve
Neighbors: Jamila & JaSun and Sabriya & Grant

It feels a little strange working today. Last year, when the planes hit the World Trade Center, we were in Boston. Now for the anniversary we're

Tonight I met up with the homeowners from the last episode for dinner.

in Washington, D.C. It's eerie how our shooting schedule worked out that way. Our producer, Laura, sensed that it might feel a little weird, so she picked up some gag gifts at the Spy Museum across the street from our hotel. She thought it would lift our spirits a little bit to have a good laugh. She gave me a pen that looks like a tube of lipstick and a blue wig. Pretty funny. It was so thoughtful of her to know that we'd all need a pick-me-up.

* September 12th, 2002
Day 2

What happened on our homeowners' block last night? There's glass all over the street from shattered car windows. *Nice.* We hope to have the crew wrapped from location before dark this evening.

Tomorrow it's off to the Emmys. I have incredible butterflies in my stomach. I am tremendously proud of our crew and show. This is going to be a phenomenal experience.

* September 13th, 2002
In Los Angeles, California, for the Emmys

3:30 p.m.
Vern and I flew out to L.A. together from D.C. We've checked into the hotel, and I've picked up my jewelry from the exchange center handling the diamonds from Fred Leighton. I couldn't believe how easy it was to get them. That $75,000 worth of 19th-century jewels was mine with only a signature. Wow!

The Century Plaza Hotel is fantastic, but there's not much time for settling in. We have to get ready for the Academy of Television Arts and Sciences reception this evening.

12:00 midnight

We were a hit at the reception. Our show was nominated as part of the Craft and Sciences Awards, so there weren't many on-camera personalities present. We were basically the biggest *"stars"* there. It was pretty cool and definitely an ego boost.

There was a short presentation of the nominations for the Craft and Sciences Awards. When the clip of Trading Spaces popped up on the screen, we heard a distinct rise in laughter and recognition for our show. It was incredibly rewarding to witness that kind of acceptance from our peers in the industry. We might be kind of a lightweight show, but it makes an impact on the viewing audience. It is empowering, it gives people great ideas they can do at home, and it brings families closer because kids and parents watch together. Being nominated means the industry notices the production values of the show. I am so proud of our team.

If it wasn't enough to take them all by storm inside the reception, we gave everyone a show outside too. I'm not sure who got the bright idea, but the next thing I knew, I was hiking up my skirt and scaling the Emmy fountain with the rest of the cast. We felt triumphant, even though we had a feeling we wouldn't actually carry home the Emmy.

* September 14th, 2002

Emmy Night!

12:45 p.m.

Patrick arrived! He came just as the brunch TLC hosted at the hotel wrapped up. The brunch was so delightful. And there was plenty of champagne! Patrick grabbed a bite and went to rest before getting ready for tonight. My makeup artist will be here in a few minutes. Oh boy. I've got butterflies in my stomach.

Ready for the Emmys

3:30 p.m.

I'm dolled up in my Carmen Marc Valvo couture and my Fred Leighton diamonds. Patrick is in his tux. I swear he looks better than me. *How do men do that?!* We're meeting everyone else downstairs to get in the limo.

I'll be in a different limo from Patrick. The spouses and dates will go separately so the cast can make a unified appearance. I will miss him. *Can't wait to go down the red carpet!* I can hardly believe this is happening. **I AM GOING TO THE EMMYS!!!!!!**

1:00 a.m.

Well, we didn't take home the winged statue, but it was a glorious experience. When they announced the nominees in our category, we received a big surge of applause for our show. The 12 seconds before they declared the winner, I thought, *"We might actually win this thing!"* Frankly, I could have done without that 12 seconds. It made it harder. But that rise in applause was priceless for a new show like ours. I was overwhelmed.

Patrick held my hand the entire night, and we watched attentively. John Cleese was hysterical. He handed out a few awards and stole the show. Most of the time, the ceremony was kind of boring. I think I stayed awake on sheer adrenaline. Patrick stayed awake because Ty kicked the back of his chair the whole time.

As we left the ceremony we were confused about where to go, but we followed the herd and wound up at a lovely party with a fabulous dinner and a great band. You can always find me on the dance floor. Even Patrick danced with me. The last time he did that was at our wedding.

I'd say the night was perfect, just because the night existed at all.

OUTSTANDING SPECIAL CLASS PROGRAM

AFI'S 100 YEARS...100 THRILLS: AMERICA'S MOST HEART-POUNDING MOVIES • CBS
Gary Smith, Executive Producer; Dann Netter, Fred A. Rappoport, Bob Gazzale, Fred Pierce, Producers
An AFI production in association with Smith-Hemion Productions

I LOVE LUCY 50TH ANNIVERSARY SPECIAL • CBS
Desi Arnaz Jr., Lucie Arnaz, Executive Producers; Gary Smith, Fred A. Rappoport, Dann Netter, Producers
Desilu Too L.L.C., Smith Hemion Productions, The Fred Rappoport Company, CBS Productions

SURVIVOR • CBS
Mark Burnett, Executive Producer; Craig Piligian, Craig Armstrong, Co-Executive Producers; Tom Shelly, Jay Bienstock, Supervising Producers; Cord Keller, Senior Producer; Maria Baltazzi, John Feist, Doug McCallie, Adam Briles, Teri Kennedy, Conrad Riggs, Bruce Beresford-Redman, Dennis Lofgren, Producers; Jeff Probst, Host
SEG, Inc.

TRADING SPACES • TLC
Denise Cramsey, Executive Producer; Susan Cohen-Dickler, Jan Dickler, Ray Murray, Executive Producers for Banyan Productions; Stephen H. Schwartz, Executive Producer for TLC; Alyssa Kaufman, Larry Blase, Aimee Kramer, Producers; Paige Davis, Host
Banyan Productions for TLC

THE WEST WING: DOCUMENTARY SPECIAL • NBC
Thomas Schlamme, John Wells, Aaron Sorkin, Executive Producers; Kevin Falls, Co-Executive Producer; Michael Hissrich, Producer; Llewellyn Wells, Anne Sandkuhler, Produced by; William Couturie, Director/Interview Materials by; Eli Attie, Felicia Willson, Interview Materials by
John Wells Productions in association with Warner Bros. Televison

The crew played poker with candy after a long day.

* September 18th, 2002
In Los Angeles

Today I did my very first talk show! I was a guest on Wayne Brady. I think it went exceptionally well. They even got me to sing. No one can do that. I'm too insecure about my voice. But Wayne was so charming, and I couldn't resist his pleas. We sang the title song from Beauty and the Beast. What chemistry! I have always been a fan of Wayne. He is so funny and talented, and now he can add the talent of talk show host to his repertoire because he does an awesome job!

* September 25th, 2002
Day 1: Fishers, Indiana
Designers: Doug & Genevieve
Neighbors: Genevieve & Craig and Dona & Brad

Dona has a serious, no-joke, all-kidding-aside phobia of feet, and she's working with Genevieve. Gen, of course, never wears shoes. She even goes barefoot in Carpentry World. Need I say anything more?

* September 28th, 2002
Day 0

I milked a cow today. Whatta ya know about that?! It's harder than you might think.

* September 29th, 2002
Day 1: Plainfield, Indiana
Designers: Doug & Vern
Neighbors: Becky & Bob and Rhonda & Mike
These kids are nuts. Love that! Harvey, our location scout, noticed something special about this place as soon as he arrived in town: the homeowners had every business on Main Street post a welcome sign. Even the movie theatre welcomed him on the marquee: **"Pick us!"** How could these teams not make the cut!

* September 30th, 2002
Day 2

I wondered for two days why Rhonda seemed so lethargic and distant. I thought maybe they roped her into "trading spaces" and she wasn't thrilled with the idea. Come to find out, she's pregnant. No wonder. My goodness, I don't know how she's managed to do all the work she's done. The first trimester is supposed to be the worst for fatigue. What a trooper. *Trading Spaces neighbors are phenomenal!*

We used a special camera today. The guys call it a "lipstick cam." It's a tiny tube camera mounted inside the race car to capture the driver's POV (point of view). We planned to have our cameraman, Andy, get into the car to operate the camera, but he's 6'4" and there was no way he could fit in that tiny space. So our audio guy, Wager, had to get in the seat—he's only 5'9". He was thrilled. Who was running audio, I don't know.

* October 1st, 2002
Day 0

We shot the Open and Designer B-roll at the Indianapolis
Motor Speedway. Wow. I learned about the "yard of bricks." The
original racetrack was made entirely of bricks. They paved over
them to create the track we see today, but left one strip of brick
exposed. It is fascinating because the brick reminds you of the
speedway's history and longstanding traditions.

* October 8th, 2002
Day 2: O'Fallon, Missouri
Designers: Genevieve & Vern
Neighbors: Jennifer & Dathan and Traci & Ric

A huge crowd of fans gathered today. At least 300 people were
out in the street watching. They couldn't understand why we
weren't able to stop midafternoon and sign autographs. Ty had it
pretty hard. Because Carpentry World is outside, the fans kept
talking to him and asking him questions. I tried to explain that
we have to finish the rooms they see on their favorite TV show.
Most of the crowd stayed until we finished taping. They waited
well over six hours to meet us and get autographs and pictures.
Those were some serious fans! Ty was exhausted and he escaped
out the back with a trash can over his head.

* October 9th, 2002
Day 0

This episode will be shot from Scott Air Force Base. Getting
on the base was a bit tricky because security is so tight, but the
military personnel made it as easy as possible. We entered

together and were escorted to the houses. They told us that we'd need to be escorted at all times when roaming the base.

I had the unique opportunity of visiting an Air Force flight strip today. Our producer arranged to shoot the Open from the cockpit of an Air Force jet. Too cool.

Even better, the Air Force gave me an appropriate outfit. They dressed me from head to toe in a flight suit with the correct patches *(with my name)*, a proper T-shirt, flight scarf, flight boots *(and socks!)*, and the final touch . . .dog tags. I was official. They even instructed me how to wear the uniform. There are many specifications: The scarf must be tucked just so, the zipper of the flight suit must be zipped up within range of the name badge, and all bootlaces and zipper tabs must be tucked in. I became such a pro that I went all over the base fixing and correcting other airmen's uniforms, making comments like *"Your uniform is not code, Sir."*

We shot the Open in two parts. The first part I sat in the cockpit alone. It felt strange. Claustrophobic, even. In the second part, I met Colonel Larry Stube at the bottom of the stairs descending from the plane. He welcomed me to Scott Air Force Base with a firm handshake. He was a natural and was so much fun. For one of the takes, he did a perfect German accent, saying, "I 'ave zee papers." We all cracked up.

October 10th, 2002

Day 1: Scott Air Force Base, Illinois
Designers: Kia & Doug
Neighbors: Bernadette & Pete and Ruth & Patrick

2:30 p.m.

We just had the distinct honor of meeting Four-Star General John Handy. He came to the set to meet the homeowners and visit the crew. It was almost surreal when he came down the cul-de-sac in front of Doug's house. The entire neighborhood stopped and stood at attention. Of course, his stature and authority didn't stop us from putting him on camera. Hey, he's in our camp now.

We had him enter the room and react to the fact that Doug was installing an actual car in the house—military housing, mind you—oh boy, talk about against code . . .

General Handy was fabulous, a real pro, and such a good sport. When we were in the scene, I introduced him to the homeowners and then tried to trick him with an old military tradition of *"coin checking."* Our homeowners tipped me off to this tradition. It seems every military unit has a distinctive coin. Military personnel design them for identification, honor, or recognition, or to commemorate a special event. Enlisted persons might have many coins, but they must carry at least one with them at all times. If you're challenged to show your coin and you don't have it with you, *you lose, and you buy the drinks.*

So there I am in the scene with General Handy, armed with my coin from the 375th Air Wing, ready to surprise him and, hopefully, win the "coin check." I wait for the perfect moment . . . "General, I have really been enjoying my time here on base. I've been made to feel like part of the family and I've been educated on some of the traditions. And I've been given some very special items to help make me an honorary member of the Air Force. Soooo, I'm just hopin' you've got yours, 'cause I've got mine!" Bam. I pulled out my coin. All the other military personnel in the room pulled out their coins with the same swift movement. Then with the most calm, deliberate, and smooth motion, General Handy reached into his pocket. As if in slow motion, totally hamming it up for the camera, he pulled out his gorgeous, heavyweight coin for all of us to see. Bam. *"Of course you have* your coin!!!!! You do not rise to be a four-star general without carrying your coin! You da man!" I exclaimed, flabbergasted and yet not at all surprised. He asked me, "You know what that means, don't you?" I responded with a pouting grimace of defeat, "Yes, I have to buy drinks." General Handy looked me in the eye with a menacing grin and requested, of all things, a nice hot cup of tea. How sweet is that?!

4:40 p.m.

Jacque, our escort, told me that if I wanted to deliver a cup of tea to General Handy, I had to do it right away because she found out that he's leaving for Afghanistan in 20 minutes!! Holy mackerel. She ran into the house with me and we scrounged around, looking for tea. I wanted to deliver a special blend of tea tomorrow, but on this deadline, ordinary tea would have to do. Ruth had a collection of porcelain teapots and teacups, so we stole (I mean, borrowed) a cup and pot from her cupboards and boiled some water in the microwave. We were outrageously comical, opening and closing cupboards, bumping into each other, and banging dishes. If only General Handy could have seen the disorderly way we prepared that cup of tea. While waiting for the water to boil I signed a publicity postcard - "Every good airman pays his debts. Love, Paige Davis." Jacque and I put the tea on a tray (also stolen—I mean borrowed—from Ruth's house), and without even telling my producer we were leaving, we jumped in the car and had Sergeant Peterson drive us

*More cool stuff
I learned on
the base:*

The order of ranks:

2nd Lieutenant – Gold Bar (otherwise known as a butter bar)

1st Lieutenant – Silver Bar

Captain – Two Silver Bars

Major – Gold Oak Leaf

Lt. Colonel – Silver Oak Leaf

Colonel – Full Bird, American Crest (eagle with arrows)

Brigadier General – One Star *

Major General – Two Stars **

L. General – Three Stars *** (known as Little General)

General – Four Stars ****

Be – Brigadier

My – Major

Little – Lieutenant

General – General

to General Handy's
office.

I witnessed something very special today in General Handy.
It is a very rare person who can live in the moment and be
present with what's happening around him without being
preoccupied with his own agenda and pending issues. General
Handy embodies that quality, and I firmly believe it is what
has enabled him to become such an influential leader. Earlier,
on set, none of us had any idea that he had a major crisis
developing that would require him to leave the country
immediately. This is a four-star general, with a tight schedule
booked in 15-minute intervals. Yet, when he was with us on set,
or with me in his office, he behaved as if we were the only
appointments in his date book. Not only is that very healthy, it
shows class.

After I delivered my tea to General Handy, he suggested I
visit his other office so I could see his coin rack. **Goodness!!!!**
He has hundreds of coins, and he presides over all of those
units. I was amazed and more than a little impressed.

✳ October 15th, 2002

Day 1: Kirkwood, Missouri
Designers: Frank & Edward
Neighbors: Karen & Bob and Judy & Ben

© Marc Jeff Schirmer

✳ October 16th, 2002

Day 2

8:30 a.m.

We shot the Open on a casino boat looking toward the St. Louis Gateway Arch. Our cameraman, Mark, decided that the shot would look better from the vantage point of the far end of the boat, and I mean the FAR end. Even the folks from the casino boat were leery of us going so close to the edge. I got the distinct impression that no other camera crew had ever tried to get a shot from that location. That didn't stop us. We just went for it. And I prayed that I wouldn't fall into the water.

Happy Birthday to me! Our executive producer, Denise Cramsey, sent me flowers like the ones I had at my wedding. They are so beautiful.

* October 20th, 2002
Dallas, Texas, with Patrick

I did a photo shoot for the Trading Spaces book coming out in March. I wore my "Roxie" costume from when I understudied the role in Chicago. It was exciting to do a portrait that focused on that part of my life. Just wearing the costume took me back to when I was dancing on Broadway. I have to admit that I really miss dancing. I truly enjoy hosting Trading Spaces—it's been the time of my life—but there's something different about the feeling I get when I'm dancing and performing onstage. I am transported.

* October 22nd, 2002
Traveled with Patrick to the next city of The Lion King tour. So we've left Dallas, Texas, and are now settling into his hotel in Ft. Lauderdale. It seems he and Sophie will be very happy here. They are only blocks from the beach, and all the necessities are close by too. I wish I could stay with them, but tomorrow I dash off to London! Trading Spaces is shooting an episode there to air the Saturday after Thanksgiving. It was devised as a way to top the Changing Rooms (the British version of Trading Spaces) marathon that TLC will air on Thanksgiving Day. If we go to London now, the episode will come out of post-production in time to be promoted during the marathon. Folks can watch the British show Changing Rooms on Thanksgiving, then see a British Trading Spaces later that weekend! Excellent.

*October 21st, 2002

My little Maltese, Sophie, was a real star today. After I recorded some voice-overs at a local studio, I went back to Patrick's hotel for a photo shoot with <u>Pet Life</u> magazine. Sophie was such a good girl. I was unbelievably proud of her. I can't wait to see the cover.

Being a diva is exhausting.

In the driver's seat of the cab . . . . and seeing
London from a double-decker bus . . . .

* October 23rd, 2002

Travel to London

11:30 a.m.

I flew all night and arrived in London in the morning. So
voilà, it's October 24th. I went straight to the hotel in a black
cab. I couldn't believe how expensive it was. The dollar does not
go very far in Britain these days. The taxi ride was over $60.
Whoa! At least the driver knew how to get to my hotel. I can't
imagine how steep the fare would have been if he had to search
around. As soon as I arrived at my hotel, I immediately put on my
makeup because Hildi, Genevieve, and I are shooting the promos
for the episode today.

6:00 p.m.

The producers of the promos rented a double-decker bus for
the shoot. It was a great idea. We had an incredible vantage

point from the top of that bus. I was particularly glad because driving around the city taping those promos was my only real chance to see London (*and I do mean see London*). We drove past Parliament, Big Ben, Piccadilly Circus, the Tower of London, and even went over Tower Bridge. I would have loved to see the Crown Jewels (*among other things*), but it was wonderful to take in the feel and look of the city. This is my first trip to London, so even seeing the streets was a big deal to me.

As we drove through the streets a few, very few, people recognized the three of us and called out to the bus. We were surprised, because although Changing Rooms airs in America, Trading Spaces doesn't air in Britain. But the people who recognized us were American tourists—they shouted out, "We're from Chicaaaago!"

Now I'm getting ready to go to dinner with the gang. My producer is going to drop off a sweater he wants me to wear in the episode. He went straight to Camden Market to buy it when he got off the plane. Nothin' like planning ahead!

7:00 p.m.

The sweater is adorable. It's a navy blue turtleneck with the Union Jack on the front. Good job, Larry. I love it.

* October 25th, 2002

Day 0

Dinner last night was at Zorba's, a quaint Greek restaurant down the street from the hotel. I'm actually a little embarrassed to talk about what happened after dinner. Let's start with the fact that our cameraman, Rob, was mooning us through a phone booth. *Can we all say, "Eight carafes of wine"?* The waiter just kept bringing them and we kept drinking them.

We ordered a "group special," where the cook decides what to serve to the table and we just ate and drank whatever was set in front of us—course after course of meat and drink. I managed to gorge myself, and indeed managed to make myself very sick. When I got back to my hotel room, it was a very brief time before I vomited. The real kicker is that I vomited all over the blue Union Jack sweater I had laid out on the bed before going to dinner. I didn't know what to do. But there was only one option: I had to clean the sweater before my call-time the next morning. So this morning *(during the only 3 hours I would have had free to do some sightseeing)* I am seeing a Laundromat. I'm looking around now. Yep, a Laundromat in London is basically the same as in the States. So much for seeing Buckingham Palace, the changing of the guard, and the Crown Jewels! Oh well.

5:30 p.m.

To get the shots for the Open and the Time's Up, we are using the same double-decker bus that was used for the promos. The view is incomparable. Rob got the greatest shot of me in front of Parliament. Truly stunning. And we did the Time's Up in front of, what else, Big Ben. So cute.

* October 26th, 2002

Day 1: London, England
Designers: Hildi & Genevieve
Neighbors: Laura & Moray and Kim & Jovo

12:10 p.m.

The rooms are underway. The British crew is fantastic. We already feel like family. They've been giving us lessons on the local colloquialisms. My favorite is *"She's got a chest like a photo finish from a Zeppelin race."* And as one might expect, there are

Hildi cleans the paint off herself.

some different names for things over here too. At one point this morning, Hildi called out for spackle. She kept calling for it, but none of the production assistants moved to get it from the cart. It turns out none of them knew what on earth she was talking about and just hoped someone else would get it. Eventually she exclaimed in desperation that those darn holes needed to be filled. A loud sigh was audible from the entire crew, "Ohhhhh, you mean Pollyfilla." (*Not Pollyfiller, mind you. They actually spell it like it sounds with their accent. Pollyfilla.*)

That cracks me up. Let's see . . . some other fun ones: *The folks on the set that we call grips? They call 'em sparks. It makes sense because they're responsible for the lights and electronics.*

* *On Changing Rooms, their Carpentry World is referred to as The Gazebo.*

* *A portable vacuum is a hoover. Any vacuum is a hoover—it doesn't matter what size—and it can also be used as a verb.*

* *baseboards = skirting*

* *molding = coving*

* *penny nails = pins*

* *Allen wrench = Allen key*

* *vice grips = mole grips*

* *And the crew didn't spare us the info that "takin' a pee" is a slash.*

12:30 p.m.

Hell must have frozen over, because the day has come when **Hildi got paint on her clothes!!!!** *Amazing, but true.* Actually she did it on purpose, so maybe it doesn't count as such a phenomenon. Hildi's plan in the little girl's bedroom involved splatter-painting the walls with eight different colors. And, as you can imagine, when the paint started flyin' the fun started getting out of hand. To see Hildi covered in paint was a historical moment.

* October 27th, 2002
Day 2

Today is my first wedding anniversary. I miss Patrick very much, but we have a lovely celebration planned for tomorrow when I meet up with him in Ft. Lauderdale.

8:00 a.m.

Our fears have come to pass. The inclement weather we'd been warned of came through last night in quite a fury—90-mile-per-hour gale force winds racing through jolly ol' England. We arrived on set to find that The Gazebo had blown over a wall and into the next yard. First order of business: Get that thing back up. I'm not sure why, though, because the winds have not died down at all. It's even difficult to walk. It feels like you're pushing against a wall the whole time.

11:00 p.m.

Overall, the entire episode came together really well, but the sheer fact that we were in London put a lot of pressure on all of us for the show to be special. We all really looked forward to shooting the show and our adrenaline was pumping. Needless to say, we basically crashed in the lobby of the hotel after we wrapped. The British crew came by the hotel too, and we celebrated together. It was nice to just relax with them for a little while.

* October 28th, 2002

Travel Day

I'm on my way back to the States, feeling extremely lucky to be on a flight today. Due to the bad weather yesterday, all the flights out of Heathrow Airport were cancelled. When I arrived at the airport today, I found myself in line with the hundreds of people who had been on those cancelled flights and were trying to fly standby today. I felt sorry for those people because I couldn't imagine any of them getting a flight anytime too soon. I would have been terribly sad if that bad weather had come through today instead of yesterday because my flight would have been cancelled, and Patrick and I wouldn't be able to have our anniversary celebration.

12:35 a.m.

Patrick picked me up at the airport, and we headed down to Miami for our mini anniversary trip. He's arranged for us to have a room at a small, quaint hotel, the St. Michel. He read all about their friendly service, and the restaurant has received rave reviews. I'm so happy to be with him, if only for a couple of days. Because my flight was late due to all the delays, we were

85

RESTAURANT
ST. MICHEL
& HOTEL

GAINZA 85

going to be very late for our dinner
reservations. I called the hotel to tell them we'd be tardy. They
were gracious and understanding. They knew we were celebrating
our anniversary and told us to only worry about being in love.
They would make sure our table was ready. *Soooo sweet!*

When we got to the hotel, we checked in and went to our room to
exchange gifts. The first anniversary is paper, so I gave Patrick
a book called ~~Living Happily Ever After: Couples Talk About
Lasting Love.~~ It told the stories of many couples with long-
lasting marriages. Each couple talked about their life together
and how they think they made it through all those years.
Accompanying the book was a letter I wrote that told our story
as if we had already made it through 50 years. He cried when he
read the part about us having a daughter.

Then he gave me my gift. It was wrapped so beautifully with
ribbons that were the colors in our wedding. He thinks of
everything. It was a strange shape, very large and flat.

I couldn't even imagine what it was. I unfolded it like a book and saw that it was two pieces of board. I saw writing, but didn't realize at first what I was seeing. Then it hit me. I gasped. He had our vows written by a professional calligrapher.

October 29, 2002

I was holding the pages flat on my lap and I was so moved that I started to cry. Patrick grabbed the pages, saying frantically, "Don't cry on them! Don't cry on them!" Then he started to cry again, so he had to quickly get them out of his own hands too! He dropped them to the floor and we both started laughing uncontrollably. We felt so close. It was good to be together again.

We still had dinner reservations ahead of us. By now we were so late it was almost ridiculous, but the restaurant did indeed have our table ready and they were incredibly nice. The dinner was absolutely delicious. We shared a bottle of champagne and the waiter surprised us with a chocolate soufflé for dessert. How sweet is that?! The whole night was dreamy.

Day Off... *Patrick and I were very lazy today. We had room service deliver breakfast and we got a late checkout from the* hotel. Once again, they were more than accommodating. "No hurry, no worry. Take your time, lovebirds." You'd think they were cunningly plotting for a grandchild.

We spent the afternoon walking along South Beach, but we could only take so much. The heat was really oppressive. I saw Versace's house. It was a little creepy knowing that he was killed on the steps right outside his gate. I was surprised when I saw just how close to the street his house sits.

* October 31st, 2002

Day 0

I was in the Admirals Club at the Dallas-Fort Worth airport during a layover on my trip to the next Trading Spaces city when I ran into Bruce Johnson, a member of The Beach Boys. He didn't recognize me at first; it had been over seven years since we'd seen one another. I reminded him that I danced with the band on tour back in the summer of '95. Then his face softened as he realized who I was. He hugged me and told me I looked great. He said the strangest, yet most telling, thing to me, *"I didn't recognize you with the smile."* I was going through a divorce when I was dancing with the band and I was very sad, but I didn't realize that I hardly ever smiled. It was a remarkable flashback for me.

* November 1st, 2002

Day 1: Madison, Mississippi
Designers: Laurie & Hildi
Neighbors: Susan & Julius and Danielle & Jay

This is Laurie's first show back since her maternity leave. Her son, Gibson, is on location with her because she's still nursing. He's beautiful and very sweet-tempered. I can't get enough of him. I

9:44 a.m.
While unloading the bedroom with Laurie's team, we discovered a dead frog under the bed! It was petrified and crispy. Eeeeew. We were so squeamish. But can you blame us? How long had that frog been there anyway?!

4:50 p.m.
We all paused for Laurie to nurse Gibson. I went upstairs to watch and talk. I sat down on the floor and rolled onto Gibson's mat, which was appropriately covered in pee. Next thing I knew, I had a hairdryer to my butt. How glamorous.

want to hold him all the time. I keep stealing him away from his nanny.

10:23 a.m.

As if it wouldn't have been exciting enough to do a bathroom for the first time on Trading Spaces, Hildi has to kick it up a notch by stapling 6,000 silk flowers all over the walls. I thought the crew was exaggerating when I overheard them talking about it in the lobby of the hotel this morning, but I just realized that is exactly what Hildi is planning to do. Oh boy.

12:35 p.m.

We headed to the governor's mansion in downtown Jackson, Mississippi, to shoot the Open. And we met Governor Musgrove. We even put him on camera. I'm beginning to see a trend with our group—it doesn't matter how important you are in the world, a governor or a four-star general, we'll try to use you in our show. The governor was very kind. Each time a man in a suit came outside we asked if that was the governor. To our surprise and delight, Governor Musgrove was the man who appeared in khakis and a button-down. He hoped we were impressed with their little capital city, though he said he doesn't see Jackson as a little city, but more as a big small town.

* November 2nd, 2002
Day 2

I did the coolest thing today: A fellow Discovery Networks employee asked me to videotape an introduction that would set the stage for him to propose to his girlfriend. I thought the idea was enchanting and felt so honored to have the task. Denise asked one of our cameramen on location to shoot it for me. I recited the script, and everyone got tears in their eyes. I just hope it's as moving for the girl who's being asked.

November 3rd, 2002
Day 0

Best laid plans, as they say: The local camera crew from Jackson has access to a jib camera. You've probably seen these in documentaries that follow the making of a film. This type of camera is an amazing apparatus. It floats through the air with grace and agility and can swoop in from above like a bird. The plan was to shoot the Open for this episode from the steps of the capitol with the jib, but as is so often the case on Trading Spaces, the weather thwarted our plans. The rain doesn't look like it will ever let up. We would definitely have time to return to the capitol steps tomorrow during Day 1, but not enough time for the crew to set up the jib. It takes about 45 minutes to get that thing mounted.

This is Patrick's first assignment producing for Trading Spaces. I know he had high hopes for such an impressive Open, but he will have to settle for an Open in the neighborhood if he wants to use the jib at all. If the camera crew is close to the location, they have time to set up the jib during breaks from shooting inside the house. Personally, I'd rather get the Open on the steps of the capitol, even though it would mean not using the jib. But these boys and their toys. Goodness. They have their minds made up.

10:45 p.m.

Laurie's parents, Janet and Richard, hosted a wonderful dinner at their house tonight for the entire crew. It was incredibly generous of them. I was really blown away by how fabulously their house is decorated—truly jaw-dropping. The food was catered and **DELICIOUS!!** They set tables throughout the house so guests could gather in smaller groups that allowed for more intimate conversation. The group at my table started listing our favorite movies. Soon we were simply listing the best movies of all time, period. The whole conversation was peppered with the **"oooohs"** and **"aaaahs"** of acknowledgment when someone mentioned a film we all agreed was legendary.

* November 4th, 2002

Day 1: Ridgeland, Mississippi
Designers: Hildi & Laurie
Neighbors: Shannon & Diane and Debby & Bob

12:34 p.m.

The crew went ahead and set up the jib camera in the cul-de-sac. It's not an impressive backdrop, but the shot should look really cool. Although I hope it isn't so different from how our show normally looks that it turns off the viewing audience. I believe the fans like the show just as it is. I get nervous when we start messing around with things too much.

1:56 p.m.

The rain stopped long enough for us to tape the Open, but that is the extent of our luck today. The rain has been very persistent and it will not let up for an extended period of time. This is the kind of weather that makes Amy Wynn, Ty, and Eddie want to pull their hair out. The carpentry tent is wet, the wood is wet, the tools are wet, and their shoes are wet. But like everyone else, they're hanging in there and making it work.

*November 5th, 2002

Day 2

The locals have been clueing us in on some colloquialisms. Southerners really know how to phrase things. **These are some of my favorites:**

"Whatcha know good?" – to which someone would reply . . ."Don't know it if it is."
"I reckon."
"We're fixin' to have ourselves a good time."
"Your mom and 'em."
"Darn tootin'."

*November 6th, 2002

Travel to NYC

Hildi, Amy Wynn, and I needed to catch a very early flight to

NYC. We'll be meeting up with Doug to shoot the print ad for a special episode of Trading Spaces in Las Vegas that will air LIVE on January 18th. The Open will be **LIVE**; then the show will cut to previously recorded tape of the work completed over the past two days *(tape that will have been frantically edited as the work progressed)*. Then each Reveal will air **LIVE**.

Needless to say, there is going to be a big publicity push, starting with this print ad. I only have one day available in my schedule for this photo shoot, so that's why we had to fly out at the crack of dawn. I have to be able to get to NYC, shoot the picture, and make it back to the airport to fly to LA tonight, because tomorrow I'm doing a second appearance on The Wayne Brady Show. Goodness.

11:30 a.m.

Murphy's Law is in full swing today. Our connection to NYC was cancelled. We didn't even know it at first! We were grabbing a bite to eat at a cafe across from our gate when we realized no one seemed to be gathering to board. *"Hmmm? Where is everybody?"* we thought. We checked the departure monitor and saw our flight had been cancelled. We had no idea why. Our only other option was to try and get on the flight scheduled to depart the hour before our original flight. We ran to the customer service desk, practically out of breath. We received seat assignments for the other flight and took off running again to get to that gate on time. The service representative prodded us to hurry, shouting in an encouraging tone, *"You're gonna miss the plane. Hurry! Hurry!"*

We did make the flight, but as you probably predicted, our bags did not. This isn't as big a deal for Amy Wynn and Hildi because they're spending the night in NYC and will have time for their bags to be delivered to their hotel. I, on the other hand, have to fly to LA this evening. If my bags don't make it to NYC before I have to leave for LA, I could be in a very uncomfortable predicament. But I can't worry about it now. The three of us are very late for the photo shoot. We filled out the paperwork at the baggage service counter and headed to the city. Hildi called Doug and told him to have champagne ready. She's a woman after my own heart. *Champagne cures all woes. It can turn any situation into a celebration. There's something in the bubbles.*

3:00 p.m.

I've been tracking my luggage all afternoon and I've just been told that it's arrived at La Guardia Airport. Now my dilemma is to figure out if there is enough time for my bags to make it into the city before I go back to the airport. To make matters even more crazy, my bags are with Delta Airlines at La Guardia, but my flight to LA is with American Airlines out of Kennedy.

I'm in the middle of this Vegas promo photo shoot. I can't be on the phone working this out. I decide to enlist the help of Stephen Schwartz. I can't believe I'm actually asking the executive producer from TLC to make my phone calls, but darned if he doesn't come through for me. Like the most efficient personal assistant, he gets on that phone and works out this incredible plan to have a car service pick up my luggage from Delta at La Guardia and meet the car dropping me off at American out of Kennedy. **It worked!!!!!** I grabbed my bags, went to check in, and made it on the flight to LA with my luggage accompanying me. He may be an executive producer now, but those days working his way up as a field producer came shining through this afternoon.

*November 7th, 2002

Arrived in LA last night and checked into the Century Plaza

Hotel. I love staying here because it's a Westin, which means there is a feather bed, a fabulous double showerhead, and the best towels ever—you know, ones that are soft AND absorbent. I don't want to leave, but I've gotta get over to The Wayne Brady Show. My friend Risa is going to join me. She's a TV producer so she knows some people who work with Wayne Brady.

6:00 p.m.
Wayne Brady was fun. I wore the Richard Tyler evening gown I wore to the Daytime Emmys! I followed Halle Berry on Wayne's show, so I did it as a joke, saying, *"Well, Wayne, you put me on your show following the single most beautiful woman on the planet. What was I supposed to do? I had to top Halle Berry."* **Hilarious!**

* November 8th, 2002
Day 0

Early-morning flight to San Antonio for the next series of Trading Spaces shoots. **Unbelievable!** On the first leg of my flight to San Antonio, I saw an old acquaintance, a dance teacher, from Los Angeles. The strangest thing is he had been on my mind for a few weeks. Right before I went to London, I received a phone call from Laird, who works with on-air promotions at Discovery Networks. She told me her idea of doing a commercial for the Vegas LIVE Reveal that would be a musical production number. She could picture me with dancing boys and the whole bit. *I was absolutely thrilled!!!* She said we would shoot the spot in LA. I immediately started thinking about who would choreograph. I knew that whatever "boys" were hired to be in the promo with me would be dancing for peanuts, so I felt that the choreographer should be someone positive and fun and who could make the experience really enjoyable for the guys. Doug

3:30 p.m.

Wouldn't you know it: my luggage didn't make my connection AGAIN! Goodness! But all the frustration melted away when I arrived at yet another Westin. The hotel is beautiful! I noticed they had a spa, so I checked to see if I could get an appointment for anything. Why bother going up to my room?! I don't have any luggage to unpack. I just went straight to the spa. Much more fun to wait for my bags while getting a massage, don't ya think?! When I finally did make it into my room—with luggage in hand—I noticed someone had delivered a gift to my room. It was a Texas-shaped box made of chocolate and filled with chocolates. It was one of the neatest things I'd ever seen. How do they do that?!

Caldwell is just that kind of man. I used to take his dance classes all the time when I lived in LA. He was so encouraging and such a good teacher. He gave his heart to his students, and his classes kicked butt! I knew he would be the perfect person to involve in this project. Problem: I had no idea how to get in touch with him. I hadn't seen him since I lived in LA over eight years ago. And it's not like we were best friends or anything. Heck, I didn't even know if he would remember me at all. Laird told me that the producer who would be working on the promo had some connections of his own in LA, so I didn't put much energy into pursuing Doug further. Well, wouldn't you know it—after no contact with him for eight years, I boarded my plane today and there he was! I pointed at him in disbelief and said, **"No way!"** *(He thought he was sitting in my seat or something.)* I reminded him of my name and I saw his face slowly take on the expression of recognition. I told him all about Trading Spaces and the idea for the musical production number. Before they could shut the gate to our flight, I

called Laird. *"I know who should choreograph the Vegas promo. Trust me. It's fate."*

Hildi did a record-album theme in her room, so I made up a record label for the Time's Up.

Hildi's room reflected in a convex mirror.

*November 9th, 2002

Day 1: San Antonio, Texas
Designers: Hildi & Vern
Neighbors: Laura & Carlos and Dana & Lynette

2:56 p.m.

I gave my good MAC powder brush to Vern and his team so they could work faster on their gold-leafing project. Vern only had one fluffy brush, so that meant only one person at a time could lay down the gold leaf. I doubled their work rate by giving them my brush. Hey, anything for the cause.

*November 10th, 2002

Day 2

We shot the Open at San Antonio's famous Riverwalk. This place is so cool. It's kind of like a Southwestern version of Venice; all the restaurants and shops are along both sides of the river and you can even take gondola rides up and down.

We were there for quite a while, looking for a place to shoot the Open. I don't think the producer for this episode entirely grasped how popular the Riverwalk is with the tourists and locals. She scouted the area the other day in the morning, before any of the restaurants and shops were open, but we were shooting the Open today, midafternoon, on the Sunday of Veterans' Day weekend. Needless to say, it was packed! We looked all over for a remote spot or at least a calm spot. And just when we thought we'd found an OK position, a mariachi band started playing. We couldn't have the music in the background because of copyright laws. We had to move again. When we set up at another location, we found ourselves at the mercy of the people in the gondolas who would be shouting out, *"We love Trading*

Spaces" or "_Hey, that's Paige Davis_" or "_Oh my God, I love that show._" Meanwhile, back at the ranch, as they say, the teams were wrapping up the finishing touches in their rooms and we were missing it all. We slammed out as many takes on camera as we could and rushed back to the houses to capture the rooms coming together. **Whew!**

*November 11th, 2002

Travel Day

I got another massage at the Westin before heading to Austin for our next series of shoots. I just couldn't resist. I can't believe how incredible I feel. Wow.

I laid down voice-overs at my favorite recording studio today. Banyan Productions used 501 Post last year when we were in Austin for the Natalie Maines episode. This place is so much fun because the decor is amazing. It's so homey and eclectic. Each editing suite is like a fully decorated living room. You really could just move in! And they always have fresh cookies baking along with other snacks: crackers, mixed nuts, candy bars, pretzels. **The way to my heart is definitely through snacks!**

7:00 p.m.

I met up with good friends, Nick and Sindy, who live in Austin. Nick is an American Airlines ticket agent I met the day I was flying home from the Natalie Maines shoot. Actually it's an "amazing, but true" story how we became friends. I lost my wedding rings in the Admirals Club at the Austin airport. He not only organized a search party, he got on a plane and hand-delivered the rings to me so there was no risk of them getting lost in the mail. I know you might think he did this just

Live entertainment (and competition for taping the Open) on San Antonio's Riverwalk

A quiet background for the Open.
Cookies from a fan...love those snacks!

Shot the Open
and Designer
B-roll at a
great vintage-
sign shop.

because he was a fan of Trading Spaces, but he hadn't even watched the show much at the time. He did it just because he's a caring, thoughtful, giving man. I know that you don't let people like that escape from your life. I have stayed in touch with him ever since.

They took me to Country Line BBQ. That was some darn fine BBQ. Austin is known for their BBQ and this place ranked right up there. Plus it had pretty colored lights. That makes any place fabulous in my book.

* November 12th, 2002

Day 0

We're hitting the halfway mark of our season with this episode, number 30 of 60. Denise is in town and she's going to take all of us to dinner to celebrate.

Later

Restaurant recommendation: Gumbos. The seafood is terrific! We got pretty noisy at the restaurant. When we all get together to relax, the laughter starts pouring out, especially when Denise is around. She is so funny. Many of the folks I work with are really funny. Sometimes I think it's our only saving grace when time is tight and moods are tense on the set. We often get rowdy and loud when we start up with jokes and begin reflecting about our ongoing Trading Spaces dilemmas and trials. Tonight was no exception. I felt bad because even though it wasn't a chichi, quiet restaurant, there was a couple near us trying to have a romantic dinner. I went to their waitress, gave her my credit card, and arranged to pick up their bill. Then I sat back down at my table and proceeded to laugh my head off again, but I didn't feel nearly as guilty about it.

This night will go down in history with all of us as the night

Kevin spit water on Denise. Everyone's gotta have a last day, Kevin.

*November 13th, 2002

Day 1: Austin, Texas
Designers: Hildi & Laurie
Neighbors: Laura & Steve and Diane & Bryan

I think Laurie may have made behind-the-scenes history today. She was unloading supplies from her car, trying to manage Gibson at the same time. Instead, she accidentally dropped one of her lamps into the street drain. The whole crew came outside to see if the lamp could be rescued. *(It hadn't fallen all the way down.)* Next thing I know, Gary, Patrick, and Kevin are all trying to come up with an engineering plan—short of using chewed gum—that would be brilliant enough to recapture this lamp. I got the entire event on Paige Cam. It was comical watching these three grown men, flat on their stomachs, stretching with all their might to reach the lamp. They tried using conventional tools. They tried using <u>un</u>conventional tools. And much to Laurie's relief they were able to recover the lamp. Unfortunately, the recovery mission was not without sacrifice: Kevin lost his watch!

*November 16th, 2002

12:23 a.m.
Nick and Sindy picked me up for an evening out on the town. Our night began with dinner at Castle Hill Café. It was a wonderful restaurant, and we got in just before the big dinner

rush. Good thing we did, too, because I would have hated to miss what came next! Nick and Sindy took me to a local comedy show, Esther's Follies. This show is known as a must-see for all visitors to Austin, and I can certainly understand why. A political musical review of sorts, it had me laughing so hard, my side ached and tears were running down my face. I've been to Austin a

Me, Nick, and Sindy on 6th Street

number of times and don't know why I never knew about this show. I can guarantee you, I will never miss it again when I'm in town. It seemed that no one in the news was spared humiliation and mocking. Even George W. Bush wasn't safe in this Texan arena.

After the show I wanted to hang around for a few minutes so I could meet the cast. I really wanted them to know how much I appreciated their talents and originality. A few of the cast members came out into the house and were picking up trash from around the seats. One guy, Jerome, started talking to me, but he wasn't really making any sense. He was saying things like "Are you followin' me or somethin'? Hey, can't wait for you to do my house!" I thought he was just a fan trying to be funny. Fans say stuff like that to me all the time. He kept talking, and I kept thinking he was a little off his rocker. Then it finally dawned on us. He thought I knew who he was—he was one of the participants on an upcoming episode in Austin. I said, "My goodness! You're the comedian!!!" I knew there was going to be a comedian on one of our shows, but I had no idea he was in Esther's Follies. The fact that I was at the show days before we started his episode was a complete coincidence! I climbed over the chair, jumped into his arms, and gave him a big hug. We just started laughing. Well, I knew right then and there we were on the brink of a hilarious episode. I had just seen it for myself in the show. This guy was funny. Funny with a capital F. Nick and Sindy were taken by surprise too. They got a big kick out of it. Small world.

Me with the cast of Esther's Follies

For me, one of the best parts about doing _Trading Spaces_ is getting to see the little bits of Americana that pop up in the neighborhoods across the country. Today I drove into the cul-de-sac to find two adorable children with a lemonade stand. Some things never change. I had a lemonade stand when I was a kid. No doubt my mom had a lemonade stand when she was a kid. And all of us were hoping to make our fortune from our first real business. Maybe we'd make enough money for candy, or a doll, or crayons, or a bike. Or maybe we'd make enough to run away from home and live on our own. I mean, who needs grown-ups anyway? We were running entire conglomerates. How grown up is that?!

*November 17th, 2002

Day 1: Austin, Texas
Designers: Kia & Frank
Neighbors: Suzi & Guido and Anu & Uttam

11:43 a.m.

I'm not sure why we're doing it, but we've set up a piece of glass to be painted while the camera catches the paint going on from the other side. I think it's just for the purpose of having a unique and different way to jazz up the Paint Reveal for this episode. It's taking a lot of time though.

4:12 p.m.

We shot the Open at The Oasis, a restaurant with a remarkable view. People go there to watch the sun set over Lake Austin.

* *November 18th, 2002*
Day 2

Neither Kia nor Frank had demanding carpentry projects for their rooms, so Ty is actually finished with all his work! He has absolutely **NOTHING** to do for these rooms today! Most crews would jump up and celebrate such an event. They'd be thrilled for the chance to slack off and relax for once. Not this group. They've decided to clean the entire trailer, the truck, and the carts—inside and out, every nook and cranny. Gary has all the tools laid out in front of him on the lawn and he is cleaning them one by one. I'm not sure this has ever been done before. It looks bizarre. Who knew we had all this stuff? It almost seems fruitless, but I admire their work ethic and dedication.

* *November 19th, 2002*
Day 0

This turned out to be quite a packed day.

Radio interviews all morning.

Then we shot the Open. This is the episode with Jerome, so we did the Open at the theater for Esther's Follies. Natalie, the lead producer on this episode, had Doug as a magician and Genevieve as his assistant sawing Ty in half. Very clever. There was a bit of a problem, though. Ty didn't fit in the box, not when it was together anyway. We could shoot his bottom half in the box and then his top half in the box, but not his whole body in the box. I thought, why not use a stunt double for the magic trick? Gen, Doug, and Ty were all in wigs, so I suggested they put Kelle, our makeup artist, in Ty's wig. That's exactly what we did. She was small enough to fit in the box. Ta da!

I did a quick change of clothes because today I shot the

Every
magician
should have
Kelle up his
sleeve.

The magician
and his
assistant

How many things can I pack into one day?

footage for the introductions to the clips for the Trading Spaces, Best Of DVD. I hope the DVD comes out well. I wonder what clips they'll choose for each section? I have my favorites, but who knows if they'll make the cut.

I found out midday that I needed to go back to 501 Post to record two lines of voice-over. An episode went through a few more changes, so we made some last-minute alterations to the voice-overs too. We actually tried to redo these lines in a bedroom with blankets draped over C-stands to create a booth. No good. I guess those soundproof booths serve their purpose after all.

I love it when my days are this busy. I was pretty tired, though. But that didn't stop me from meeting the gang at the Malibu Grand Prix. It was worth it just to see Andy fit into a race car, instead of getting stuck like he did at the Indianapolis Motor Speedway.

Finally, a race car Andy can fit into.

Jerome bares all in Carpentry World...

*November 20th, 2002

Day 1: Austin, Texas
Designers: Doug & Genevieve
Neighbors: Courtney & Eric and Angie & Jerome

8:05 a.m.

All right, now I've seen it all—practically literally! Last night, after the crew left for the evening, Jerome decided to bare all for some gag pictures. He got buck naked and took pictures in Carpentry World and Sewing World. We're going to have to lock up better from now on. No one should be subjected to that.

10:05 a.m.

I predicted a hilarious episode with this gang, and I was right. When Jerome, Angie, and Genevieve moved the sofa from the room during "load out," it revealed a taped outline of a figure that looked like a chalk line from a crime scene. Will the insanity ever end?

116

4:56 p.m.

Apparently not. I'm not complaining, though. I've been laughing nonstop all day. I am, however, beginning to think Jerome would prefer to go through his whole life naked. He stripped AGAIN! This time to pull a practical joke on Ty. We always tease Ty because he's basically naked everyday too (his pants are usually hanging on by a hair). Jerome decided to take this teasing to a new level, so he showed up in Carpentry World "ready to work." He figured he'd be in the right outfit—which is no outfit. He wore nothing but a tool belt with paint sample strips hanging down to cover his Johnson. Kevin stood guard so Ty wouldn't see Jerome before we were ready to capture the whole thing on camera. You didn't think we wouldn't get that on tape, did you?

12:50 a.m.

Being naked is an ongoing theme it seems. Someone decided we would celebrate Laura's birthday tonight by hiring a stripper. *This guy actually came to the Mexican restaurant and did his routine right there at the table!* He didn't get totally naked, of course, but that didn't stop Laura from turning eight shades of red.

November 21st, 2002

Day 2

I thought the "naked" pictures of Jerome from the other evening were so funny that I got him to show them on Paige Cam. We kind of pretended he had done them the evening of Day 1 instead of the evening of Day 0. A little creative license. Wonder if it'll make it into the episode.

10:16 a.m.

I almost forgot I had a radio interview today, but I remembered just in time and turned on my cell phone for the call. Whew!

* November 22nd, 2002

Traveled to New York today. I have a meeting at my agent's office for a potential spokesperson opportunity. This could end up being a big deal. I'm a little nervous, but I understand from my agent that the person I'll meet today is very approachable and kind.

After the meeting I will have the weekend free in New York!!! Originally I was scheduled to fly to LA this evening to shoot a skit for the VH1 Best of 2002 Awards. But TLC put the kibosh on it. They didn't feel comfortable with me doing the skit for another network. I'm not certain of all the intertwining political

aspects of that decision, but whatever. It got cancelled
last minute, but that was really my fault. I didn't approach
TLC with the skit for approval or ask permission to do it.

I got a little overzealous when my personal publicist
called me with the offer. I always put Trading Spaces first;
obviously it's my Number One priority. But when I saw in my
calendar that this VH1 skit would work out, I got carried
away. I was just thinking it was publicity—fabulous. They'd
be thrilled to reach the VH1 market. If I hadn't been so
excited, I would have realized I needed their approval.

The worst part is, I could have been in Ft. Lauderdale with
Patrick if I hadn't changed my flight plans to go to LA.

Well, all of this is neither here nor there now. I'm in New York
for the weekend, passing the time until Monday when there will
be a first-ever full-cast photo shoot! Cool. And at least I'll
get to spend time with my friends in New York.

November 23rd, 2002
Day Free!

I slept kind of late. I was tired because I cried quite a bit
yesterday. Everything happened so last minute and I was
pretty embarrassed by the whole VH1 situation. I think, too,
that it was the catalyst that unleashed the flood of emotions
I'd been keeping back because I miss Patrick so much. To be so
close to seeing him for a few days, only to lose those days for
no reason at all, was hard to swallow. I had a hard time
forgiving myself.

Now I'm going shopping, which is a very good thing. Not to
cure my woes *(though that could be a definite benefit)*, but because
I still have to find a couple of outfits for the cast photo shoot.
A wardrobe stylist will bring some options, but we are

supposed to bring
some stuff too.
Besides, it's safer
when you bring
your own clothes.
Then you're
guaranteed to
like what you'll
be wearing.

*November 25th, 2002
Cast Photo Shoot

6:00 a.m.

Call-time in the lobby. Sans makeup, sans hair: **Yikes!** I did
my hair anyway. I desperately need a haircut. Oh well, life on
the road. It's hard to get these things done.

It's weird to see the whole cast together in one place. I'm not sure
this has ever happened. We didn't even have everyone present at
the Emmys.

5:00 p.m.

The first image TLC wanted to shoot during this photo session
involved the entire cast dressed all in white, painting ourselves
into a corner with red paint. I loved this idea. I saw a
preliminary photo and thought it looked **sooooo cool.** We really
looked like we had trapped ourselves in a corner. It seemed
absolutely plausible that our cast would do that to ourselves.
Sometimes the teams work so furiously that things happen
before they even know it.

The second shot called for the cast to be in all white, but this time the designers and carpenters would be in a line—a chorus line—and it would look like I had just painted a huge red stripe across their bodies. Hee hee.

8:00 p.m.

TLC hosted dinner at The Gramercy Tavern, a restaurant I have wanted to try ever since moving to New York City. It's down in Gramercy Village, and I've always heard how fabulous the food was there. It absolutely lived up to its reputation. Even the hors d'oeuvres were special and unique. Fresh scallops with portobello mushrooms, shrimp things. Yum.

Before even trying the food, though, I was blown away by the beautifully decorated table. Roger Marmet from TLC arranged for a gorgeous centerpiece that ran the entire length of the table! The flowers were stunning and they were accented with candles and fruit. Amy Wynn liked the centerpiece too—she actually ate a crabapple from it. Roger also chose some remarkable wines to accompany our meal, but I just couldn't indulge. We have a 7:00 a.m. call-time tomorrow morning for the second day of this photo shoot.

* November 26th, 2002

Cast Photo Shoot

We did two different images today. One in regular clothes like we wear on the show, and another one with us in black evening wear. Cool.

5:30 p.m.

We've finished with the cast photo shoot, but I have to stay a little longer. Turns out TLC wants to shoot me again for the

Vegas print ad that Hildi, Doug, Wynn, and I did a few weeks ago. The original photo has me in a showgirl costume (no, not topless, but rather risqué), bare midriff, bikini bottoms with fringe, you get the idea. Apparently I looked pretty hot. Maybe a little too hot. They want to take a shot of me wearing something different, and then they'll digitize me into the photo with Doug, Hildi, and Wynn.

So now I have to stay in New York longer and can't fly this evening to see Patrick. They said they'd get me on an early-morning flight, but I can't do that either because I'm scheduled for a five-hour radio tour to publicize the upcoming London episode. I can't leave until after 3:00 p.m. I'm losing a whole day with Patrick. I feel so awful because my entire week of Thanksgiving vacation gradually whittled itself down to two days: VH1 flop, the photo shoot, and the Vegas redo. These are the days it's hard to remember how lucky I am, but I keep reminding myself.

*November 27th, 2002
Still in NYC

6:45 a.m.
I'm getting ready for this radio thing. These "tours" are kind of cool. I've done them for television too. The talent stays in one place and knocks out one interview after another. There's a mediator who negotiates all the calls and makes sure everyone is connected.

Handy Andy, the carpenter from Changing Rooms, is going to participate from London in a few of the interviews with me. Wild.

6:00 p.m.
I am finally on my way to Florida to see Patrick. We were going

123

to spend Thanksgiving Day with The Lion King cast, but because we have so little time to be with each other, we're escaping to a hotel down in Miami. *Patrick found a great hotel that allows pets, so we can even bring Sophie with us!*

I'm actually flying into Miami instead of Ft. Lauderdale, so Patrick is just going to meet me at the hotel. I can't wait to see him and Sophie.

* November 28th, 2002
Thanksgiving Day

10:00 p.m.
We had Thanksgiving dinner at the St. Michel Hotel, where we celebrated our anniversary. It was romantic to go back there. It was only a month later, but it felt nostalgic. The buffet included peeled shrimp, Patrick's favorite. He was happy. And we had champagne, of course. *It goes with everything, remember?*

After dinner we walked around South Beach. Patrick wanted me to see the Delano Hotel. **WOW!** Why do people say this place is overrated? I thought it was jaw-dropping. I was completely blown away by the decor and the architecture. We sat in one of the cabanas by the pool and just talked. I love having time to just hang out with Patrick.

What a wonderful day.

* December 1st, 2002
Day 1: San Clemente, California
Designers: Vern & Genevieve
Neighbors: Amy & Tim and Laurie & Dan

This will be a unique episode. It is the first time Trading Spaces is going to be taped in high definition. Banyan

Patrick and
Sophie: so
cosmopolitan
at the
luxurious
Loews Hotel.

Vern can laugh again, now that the spot remover is working.

Vern's feet, minus the paint-tracking boot

Productions even hired two makeup artists to be available in each house at all times. I guess in high definition you can see everything. I'm wondering if it will look any different to people who don't watch the episode on HDTV.

The camera guys are totally insane with glee. They LOVE that we're doing this. It's like they're playing in the Super Bowl or somethin'. If you can imagine hippopotamuses dancing on their tiptoes, you've got the picture. I've never seen our guys act this way, but they're actually giddy. Me? I'm just petrified I'm going to wake up tomorrow with a big zit on my nose.

I was able to see some of the footage on the monitor. It did look awesome. It was so crisp and clear and vibrant. The Open was beautiful.

5:00 p.m.
Ooops! Big Ooops!

I was helping Vern mount the diamond shapes for his padded wall. The overhead camera was rolling and, in an attempt to be entertaining, I backed up to the other side of the room and took a running leap into the padded wall. *Funny, right?* It surprised the hell out of Vern, and he laughed. He said, *"Do it again."* I ran again. We laughed again. I said, *"Hey, you do it with me."* So, both of us laughing, we took a running leap and crashed into the wall full force. We were in stitches. That is until we looked down and noticed that Vern's boot had tracked black paint onto the carpet! We went from uproarious laughter to dead silence in a split second. Vern was mortified. I was numb. He said, *"Denise is going to kill me."* I said, *"There is no reason Denise ever needs to know about this if we get it out."* *"The whole thing was captured on the overhead!"* he reminded me.

Just then, Denise walked up the stairs. We saw the tip of her head, then her face. Uh oh. She heard the whole thing: run, run,

run, BAM, *"Ha ha, do it again,"* run, run, run, BAM, *"Ha ha ha,"* *"Do it with me!,"* run, run, run, BAM, *"Ha ha."* Well, so much for Denise never finding out. I suddenly felt transported back to a time when I was sent to the principal's office. We told her we thought it would look funny on the overhead. She wasn't laughing. Vern offered to pay for any damages out of his own pocket. He offered everything short of his firstborn. I just dropped to my knees and started dousing the carpet with spot remover and water. We had to keep it wet. Our only real chance was to use a wet vac. Just keep dousing and sucking, dousing and sucking.

* December 2nd, 2002
Day 2

8:00 a.m.
The first thing I did this morning was check Vern's house to see if Amy and Tim were able to get the rest of the paint out of the carpet. They had. It looked terrific. Thank goodness.

7:35 p.m.
It was time for the first Reveal. I led Laurie and Dan up the stairs to their newly decorated loft/media room, I got them in place, and was just about ready to say, *"Open your eyes,"* when I heard shouting from Andy, our cameraman. Andy, the gentle giant. Andy, who rarely speaks, let alone screams. *"Wait! Wait! Don't open! Don't open your eyes!! I'm seeing zebras! I've got zebras! It's going crazy! Hold up! Hold up!"* What he was referring to was a zigzag effect across his viewfinder. He thought it was being recorded, thus ruining the shot. And the Reveal is the one moment we cannot reshoot if it gets messed up. Once those honest reactions happen, it would be impossible to

capture them again. Denise looked over at Guy, the man who had been handling the HD feed from the cameras. She asked if everything was okay. Guy said the feed was perfect. "Look at my monitor," he said. "That's the monitor that is true to what is being recorded." Denise exclaimed, "You don't understand. Andy just screamed. I take that very seriously." He reassured her that everything was fine. She looked at him, evaluated the situation, and decided she had to put her trust in him. She called out to Andy and Jason, the other cameraman, to carry on. Denise may have been cool and calm during Andy's moment of panic, but I guarantee she was crossing her fingers when we rolled tape again. We checked the tape afterward. Everything came out great. And Laurie and Dan loved their room to boot.

* December 3rd, 2002

Day 0

Today we're going to the beach. Too bad it's not to relax. We're going to capture the Open and the Designer B-roll out there. Larry, our producer, has arranged to have wet suits for all of us, and we're doing a surfing theme. Genevieve looks amazing in her wet suit. What a sex kitten. Her boyfriend,

Tyler (yes, the guy from Junkyard Wars on TLC), is here with her. He's got an amount of drool that I believe is appropriate when seeing your hot girlfriend in a wet suit.

Doug is not happy to be wearing his wet suit. He's not one for the whole surfing thing. He's got issues with sinuses and I think he felt weird doing it, since he was aware that Ty actually knew how to surf. Ty did indeed catch a wave.

This episode is also being shot in high definition. The ocean looks so beautiful in the monitor! We're going to get addicted to this. *TLC, can we shoot in HD all the time? Pleeeease.*

3:00 p.m.

It is imperative that I record some voice-overs today, so even though the closest post-production studio is 45 minutes away in San Diego, Denise and I have to head down there. We also have to record the voice-over spots for the "Best of" DVD.

5:09 p.m.

No offense, Ron, but the voice-over script for the DVD was kind of lame. I love ya, but it needed some doctoring.

Luckily, Denise and I were able to reach Ron by phone so we could go over some changes with him. We finally got the new DVD script recorded. Since the process took so much longer to accomplish, Denise and I were faced with the immediate threat of not making it to Fed Ex on time to drop off the recordings for the next Trading Spaces episode. It has to finish post tomorrow. If Banyan doesn't get that tape, the episode will not make its air date!

What followed was a mad dash for Fed Ex, complete with illegal traffic moves, sighs of worry, and the inevitable wrong turn. We couldn't figure out where the place was located. When we finally spotted it, we saw the Fed Ex truck pulling away. I shouted to Denise, "Block the road. Block the road. We'll head him off at the pass!" I jumped out of the van and ran to the truck. I pleaded with the Fed Ex guy, "It's not too late is it?" Denise said at one point I was on my tippy toes. He told me we had to go to the customer service center. *"But you're leaving NOW!"* He assured me it wasn't too late and there was another truck waiting to pull out after him. I signaled to Denise to drive further up. I ran beside the van like a maniac. As I was running I could hear people in the parking lot saying, "Hey, that's Paige Davis. Paige, we love your show. Paige, you're awesome. Trading

131

Spaces rocks." I flew right past all of them because my single goal was to make it through that Fed Ex door before 7:30 p.m. Just as I got to the door, I turned back to the parking lot with a sweeping gesture and grandly shouted to the people outside, *"Thanks, everybody!"* Denise looked at me like I was an idiot and then dropped her head in shame on the steering wheel. I was enjoying the thrill of the rush and the panic. It all felt like a scene in a movie.

I stood in the entrance of Fed Ex, the package in one hand, the other hand dramatically raised in the air as I asked, completely out of breath, *"Did I make it?!"* I swear the woman at Fed Ex was the only person in a five-mile radius who did not know or care about me or Trading Spaces. With a very tight-lipped expression she said, "Sorry." I begged. I told her we rushed here. I told her we got lost. I told her we put up a barricade for the Fed Ex truck. I told her the driver said it would be OK. She looked at me in disgust and reluctantly gave in. "Well, all right. This one time," she said. *I thought, "Great! We only need this one time. We'll never be back here again. Hee hee."* I thanked her profusely and graciously. I walked back outside and, with arms raised high over my head, triumphantly exclaimed to Denise that we made it!

A celebration was in order. We went to a seafood restaurant on the pier in downtown San Clemente. Doug joined us for dinner, which Denise decided would be on the company as thanks for our heroic efforts that day. It was fun to tell Doug about our escapade.

* December 6th, 2002
In Los Angeles

I traveled to LA last night. For the next few days I'll be

132

shooting commercials that will promote the upcoming LIVE Reveal from Las Vegas. Today I had a wardrobe fitting for all the promos, and now I will head to a recording studio to lay down the vocal track for the one commercial that will be a musical production number. I am ecstatic about this musical number!! I can't believe TLC wants to do this! I'm singing lyrics set to the tune of "Ragtime Doll."

We've got **designers.**
We've got **homeowners.**
We've got a **thousand clams, (but)**
We've only got **two days.**
Let's hope **Las Vegas pays (off).**

After the sewing,
After the building,
After the paint is dry,
See **how the neighbors feel**
In our **first LIVE Reveal.**

Are they gonna **love it?**
Are they gonna **hate it?**
We're gonna take you **there.**
When they open their eyes,
Be **there for the surprise!**

How cute is that?!! I'll be singing and performing along with six dancing boys. It is going to be so much fun! I just can't wait!

3:00 p.m.
Met up with the boys to rehearse the number. And it was wonderful to be reunited with Doug Caldwell. He called me Ms.

Davis and asked me what I wanted to do first. He suggested that I watch what they had created so far.

The number was fabulous! Cheezy, funny, and cute. I knew Doug was the right person for this gig. He is an amazingly talented, A-list choreographer, but he can let go of his ego and not take things too seriously. The guys were great. They quickly taught me my part. After rehearsing it a little bit, we left the dance studio and headed to the production studio to block out the dance on the set. We made some adjustments and I said good-bye. I will see them again the day after tomorrow. In the meantime, I'll be shooting the commercial promos that involve Doug, Hildi, and Amy Wynn.

* December 7th, 2002
Promo shoot day

The promos involving Doug, Hildi, and Amy Wynn are going to be really cool. We'll all be in evening wear and the spots will center on casino tables: craps, blackjack, slots, and roulette. Laird wrote some clever dialogue along the lines of *"If you're gonna trade spaces, you've gotta know the house rules."* Can we say over the top? Yes we can. I love it!!!!

I only realized today that these Vegas promos are being shot on film, as opposed to tape. Whoa, big money.

8:43 p.m.

Hildi's husband, Etienne, joined the four of us for a night out on Sunset Blvd. How Hollywood! We have been staying at the Hyatt on Sunset which has been Hollywood enough. It's known in the industry as The Hyatt Riot because all the rock stars stay here and party all night long. Hildi wanted to see the other famous hotels on Sunset. We started with dinner at Phoenix in The

Argyle Hotel. Leon Hall introduced me to this amazing restaurant when we were both in town for the Emmys. The food was great, of course, and Chef Joseph Antonishek remembered me from before. He sent over some wonderful appetizers for us to enjoy.

Our next stop—The Standard. I thought the same thing I thought the first time I went there. Cool. The decor whisks you back to old Hollywood, very retro. And they always have a live model in her underwear in a glass viewing box behind the front desk. It's always crowded but a little "too cool for school" for me. I have to admit, though, that it's a sight to see.

We stayed only briefly and then headed to The Mondrian Hotel. The architecture there is incredible. In their gift shop I found toothbrushes that looked like dancers. They could stand up on their own because the handle was a pair of legs with turned out feet. I bought six to give to my dancing boys at the promo shoot tomorrow. Speaking

Rehearsing in
the dance studio

photo by Dean Minerd

of promo shoot—I've got to go to bed. I'm really looking
forward to doing this tomorrow. I can't wait.

✳ December 8th, 2002

Promo shoot day

Dean is the director/producer for the commercials. He is
a dream to work with. He's very calm and respectful and he
listens to other people's ideas without getting offended. He
has taken to calling this musical promo **"The
Paigetacular,"** yet another reason for me to love him. I am
having the time of my life. *The boys are amazing!* I love my
costume. It's very Moulin Rouge. The boys are in top hats
and tails. Stunning. Not all of the tuxes fit the boys, but
they are such troopers. They really do look great.

It's so refreshing and comfortable to be around a group
of dancers again. Dancers are just a different breed. I
hardly know these guys, but I feel like I'm with friends
because all dancers share a common bond.

© David Travis Grieb

Poor Matt. He's the guy who has been saddled with the lifts in this extravaganza. I'm a big girl and there's no telling how many times we'll have to run this number for the camera.

Plus every time we do the final lift to the shoulder he gets a mouth full of feathers.

Much to Dean's chagrin, Laird had the brilliant idea of dropping confetti at the end of the number. Every time we do a take, the crew literally sweeps in to get all the confetti off the floor. They do it so quickly!

I can't wait to see the final edits of these promo spots. I think this has been one of the most enjoyable promo shoots TLC has done for an episode.

* December 9th, 2002

Day 1: San Clemente, California
Designers: Kia & Frank
Neighbors: Judy & Mark and Linda & Brian

These neighbors are wonderful. They're very outgoing, goofy, and crazy. They even want to make the Key Swap funny. I think because the participants on Trading Spaces are usually die-hard fans, they concoct wild schemes for the trademark moments in the show. Mark's got something going on with numerous suitcases and Judy put together a rather risqué basket of goodies she hopes will inspire Linda and Brian when they're working on her and Mark's bedroom.

* December 10th, 2002

Day 2

11:06 a.m.

Our dear sewing coordinator, Daniel, is terribly sick. He's all bundled up and huddled next to the space heater. Poor baby. I wish I could make him some matzo ball soup.

2:10 p.m.

We just shot some promo spots for TLC's Home for the Holidays: Trading Spaces marathon, which will air on Christmas Day. Even though it's 80 degrees outside, Ty, Kia, Frank, and I wore winter hats and scarves. It was so funny with the palm trees in the background. And Ty had a great idea to use sawdust as snow. It looked like sawdust, but that's what made it so funny.

4:06 p.m.

OK, what's going on?! Everyone is dropping like flies! It seems as if Daniel isn't the only one who is sick.

8:42 a.m.

Apparently Judy is quite the "BeDazzler." She attacked her Trading Spaces shirt, and it turns out she BeDazzled her way through some other items of clothing as well.

She made custom tank tops for Jeff and James, our sound guy and our grip. They have been dedicated (all of a sudden) to improving their physiques. Lately they've started a "regimen" of push-ups and sit-ups during every break between shooting scenes. She BeDazzled workout shirts for both of them, each with a "J" matching the one Judy has on her own shirt. And if that weren't enough, she made matching thong underwear for herself and Jeff. This is definitely a club I don't want to be a member of. When did she have time to do all of this? Hello, Homework!

© Marc Jeff Schirmer

© 2003 SeaWorld

Day 0

This was a day to remember. Natalie had a wonderful plan to shoot the Open and the Designer B-roll at SeaWorld. Mary Beth is a researcher for Trading Spaces at Banyan, and she looked into all the different activities the designers and I could do on camera. One of the cutest was having Amy Wynn interact with the animals from the Fools with Tools show. The look of surprise on Wynn's face was priceless when she saw Ethel the otter come around the corner with a toy mallet. I think we all fell in love with Ethel.

Then it was off to the dolphin pool, where the designers did their B-roll. Vern got to ride a dolphin! Really! And fast too! He was amazing. I was so impressed. He held on tight and let that dolphin take off at lightning speed. Now, that's some good TV.

I don't know who had more fun me playing with whales or Amy Wynn talking to Ethel.

Finally it was my turn. The Open was going to happen in front of the Shamu tank. I was introduced to Tucker and a few other trainers. They helped us orchestrate the greatest Open ever! The trainers timed the whales' movement so they would launch simultaneously into grand flips just as I finished speaking the last lines of the Open. It took my breath away. It was a good thing that the whales were so well-trained and disciplined because the trainers wouldn't have let us try too many takes. They're very respectful and protective of the whales. Even in between the five or six times we rolled tape, we had to pause to give the whales a break so they could relax and play.

The whales didn't seem to need a break, but they sure did want to play. They would sneak up behind me and thrust themselves onto the stage platform at the front of the tank. I swear they were laughing. I could see that mischievous look in their eyes. I think they pretend to be tired so the trainers will let them goof off. But they're not foolin' me.

We got in place to shoot the Time's Up. I don't know who thought of this idea, but the Time's Up involved me hugging a whale!! The trainers helped us place the whale in front of the camera, and I kneeled at the edge of the tank. The trainers taught me a signal the whale would recognize as a command to nod its head to say "yes." Basically I just had to nod my head, and then the whale would nod its head. I said to the whale, "Do you think these rooms are gonna make a splash?" The whale nodded yes. I said, "I hope so, because time's up." Then the whale shot up out of the water and I wrapped my arms around her. It was the most majestic, awe-inspiring experience of my life. I was completely overcome with wonder. This enormous, intimidating animal presenting itself in such a graceful, loving way was astonishing and magical.

142

*December 13th, 2002

Day 1: San Diego, California
Designers: Frank & Vern
Neighbors: Mary & Buddy and Kelly & Richard

7:52 a.m.

As I drove up the street this morning, I saw three adorable girls waiting to greet us as we arrived on location. They were totally decked out in matching, handcrafted "We love Trading Spaces" shirts. They looked like a girl band. Seeing their bright smiles and feeling their excitement reminded me of why I love doing this show: The fans.

11:00 a.m.

Aaaaaw man. There's a party pooper in every

bunch. Some neighbor is ticked about the noise and the intrusion on her street. She filed a complaint, and the police came to investigate. Well, it turns out that we were technically in violation of our permit.

The permit specified using the grounds of the houses only. I think we were supposed to put Carpentry World on the cement patch that ran alongside Mary and Buddy's house. Apparently the carpentry equipment didn't fit there, so it was relocated to the street, just like it has been on numerous episodes. The neighbor forced the issue and because of that we were required to move Carpentry World further up the street. Guess how far we had to move it . . . 30 feet! Yep, that's it. The entire carpentry setup had to be picked up and moved a whopping 30 feet. Now you tell me how that is going to help this woman with her issues of noise and disruption?

2:15 p.m.

I just walked into Frank's room and found Daniel, our sewing coordinator, and Mary lying on the floor, looking up at the ceiling and giggling (not accomplishing anything on the room, mind you). They cracked each other up when Daniel almost stabbed himself accidentally with a pair of scissors, and Mary commented that at least he's the guy that would know how to sew himself back up.

* December 14th, 2002
Day 2

9:35 a.m.

I know that Buddy works in an electronics store, but I found six remotes in the drawer of his coffee table. You'd think he would have access to one of those all-in-one remotes. If the guys at the electronics store can't figure those dang things out, how the heck are we supposed to know how to operate them?

3:10 p.m.

Hey, Tucker from SeaWorld is here! It's so flattering that he's a fan of <u>Trading Spaces</u> because we all have tremendous admiration for the wonderful work the trainers do at SeaWorld.

6:30 p.m.

Mary and Buddy's little girl just created a chain reaction cryfest in her house after her parents saw their finished room. When she was reunited with Mary after the Reveal, she looked at her mom so sweetly and with tears in her eyes said, "I love the room, Mommy. I'm so happy you like it too." Her reaction was so adorable that it made Mary cry. Then that made our producer, Natalie, cry. You can always count on waterworks from me, but then I noticed Vern was crying, Frank was crying, the cameramen and sound guys were tearing up, and a few reporters were wiping their eyes too. Something about <u>Trading Spaces</u> that I sometimes forget is that we can actually make an impact on people's lives.

* December 17th, 2002

Day 1: Van Nuys, California
Designers: Laurie & Genevieve
Neighbors: JT & Rick and Lisa & Teddy

Cool homeowners. Teddy is the keyboardist for Alice Cooper's band. And Rick is a musical theater baby like me.

9:01 a.m.
We went LIVE via satellite with <u>Good Day Live</u>.

1:07 p.m.
Andrea, the nanny, arrived with little Gibson. He is bigger and

cuter than ever, and guess what? He can even hold his head up on his own now.

1:34 p.m.

Lisa and Teddy just got word that their Great Dane, Bowie, was taken to the emergency veterinary hospital. He's undergoing surgery for a condition called "bloat," something that apparently can happen to big-chested dogs like Danes. The stomach fills with gas and twists up, cutting off circulation. Although Great Danes are large dogs, they have delicate systems. Lisa and Teddy think that the excitement of Trading Spaces and the trauma of going to a kennel and being separated from Teddy again so soon after he returned from a concert tour took an emotional toll on the ol' pup.

Lisa and Teddy seem to be holding up all right. I would be a mess. They are very concerned, but they are still glad to be trading spaces with their neighbors and plan on sticking with it. We are all going to pitch in at homework time so they can get over to the vet right away.

* December 18th, 2002

Day 2

7:30 a.m.

I handed out my Christmas gifts to everyone. I gave them Trading Spaces coins minted just like the military coins we saw at Scott Air Force Base. I accompanied the coin with a letter that explained the significance of the tradition, but the people who had been on the shoot at Scott AFB immediately knew what the coins were. The back of the coins read "For the triumphant accomplishment of each episode . . . I salute you."

11:41 a.m.

Laurie's rug did not arrive in the mail today, and now she's in a bit of a dilemma. We're headed to an outlet store to find a

© Kenny Fried

12:58 p.m.

Well, we made it back safe and sound from Amigo's Secondhand Rugs. Laurie found a great rug, and Kevin behaved himself behind the wheel. Thank you, Sweetie.

Much to our surprise, we returned to the houses to find Slash from Guns 'n Roses. He's hanging out and even sewing with Genevieve. Cool. He's good friends with Teddy, so he stopped by to see what all the fuss was about. He took the cutest pictures with Gibson. The pictures with Gibson, Laurie, and Slash look like a family. Can you imagine Laurie married to Slash?

replacement, and I've got the Paige Cam with me to capture all the drama. The drama going on behind the scenes, however, could turn out to be a lot worse. Kevin, our AP, is driving us to the rug store, and he is a maniac on the road. (Yes, you are, Kevin.) Our lives are in his hands. We love you, Kevin. But be careful.

*December 19th, 2002
Travel Day

12:30 p.m.
I woke with a start when I heard my cell phone ring at 9:00 this morning. As I answered the phone, I didn't even listen to who was on the other end—I was frantically trying to figure out where I was and what day it was. It suddenly hit me: I HAD OVERSLEPT!! I did remember receiving a wake-up call, but I also remembered falling back asleep. I put the pieces together. I became absolutely frantic. I hung up on Chantal because I realized I had not only overslept, I had undoubtedly missed my plane. The thought of missing that flight filled me with dread because Patrick had been generously granted four days off so he could be with me when I had time free. We have reservations in Disney World beginning tonight, and I just knew that if I missed my plane, we would lose an entire day together.

So, if you know me, you can imagine the drama, the tears, and the fretting. I was in the Valley, at least 45 minutes from the airport. The flight was at 10:30 a.m., it was already 9:00 a.m., and I hadn't even packed my bags. There was no way. I don't even know why I tried. But I guess an automatic survival mechanism kicked in. I jumped in the shower—I literally jumped in and jumped out. Soap, shampoo, go. I blew my hair dry. No brush, no nothing. Pointed the hair dryer at my head and packed my toiletries at the same time. I threw on some clothes and called the bellman. I said, "I need someone at my door in exactly ten minutes, no later and not before. And I need my car brought around from the valet—my number is 437." I proceeded to cram everything into my bags, any which way, as long as it fit. The bellman arrived in exactly ten minutes. I threw a twenty at him and said, "I need this stuff loaded in my car and I need to be checked out of my room." I packed my carry-on bag and headed for the lobby. The bellman was amazing (however fruitless the attempt would end up being). He got my car loaded and ready to go. I went from the elevator to my car without stopping. As I ran through the lobby of the hotel, the employees were shouting, "Good luck. Drive carefully, Miss Davis. Drive carefully." Yeh, yeh, yeh, screeeeeech!

While I was on the road, I called Nick and Chuck at American Airlines. They are becoming accustomed to frantic pleas for help from me. I told Chuck I was in LA, on the 405, it was rush hour, and my flight was departing in one hour. I asked if there was anything he could do. "Welcome to my world," I said. Chuck really came through for me. Even though all the flights were booked because of the holidays, he found me a seat on a flight that left two hours later. My hero. I would have been miserable if I had caused myself to miss an entire day of vacation with Patrick.

11:07 p.m.

I've landed at the airport in Tampa. Patrick will come straight from the theater to pick me up, and we'll head to Disney World! Patrick LOVES Disney but he's never been to Disney World, only Disneyland. I mean, please, anyone who's been to both knows they are not the same park. He has no idea what's in store.

Vacation

9:00 a.m.

Patrick and I are very blessed to have a personal escort taking us around Disney World over the next four days. We anticipate an extra-special experience because our escort is going to take care of all our reservations and needs. That is, however, if we ever make it over to the park. Right now it's raining extremely hard and it seems futile to fight the storm. Patrick and I have told the guide to wait until noon to see if the rain will let up. But I tell ya, even if it's still raining later on, I'm leaving. I can't wait to get inside that park!

12:00 p.m.

The weather seems to be cooperating. Yippee!! In the words of Peter Pan, "Come on everybody!"

First stop—Animal Kingdom

We went on an incredible safari. The best part—the elephants. They are my favorite animal and have always moved me with their surprising grace and agility. When we came around the corner and saw a herd of them so close to the path, I was breathless. We were about to move on to the rest of the Animal Kingdom when Chris, our guide, directed us out of the gate and turned us over to some other "cast members" from the park. They asked if I wanted to get a closer look at the elephants. Chris had arranged an unbelievable surprise. We climbed a steep metal staircase, and the next thing I knew, I was inside the safari grounds, standing on a ledge and face-to-face with an elephant! I gasped. It was amazing to be so close that I could have touched the elephant's trunk. What an honor to be brought up to this place!

Sometimes I can't believe my good fortune. First hugging a whale, then this. I have a magical life.

* December 30, 2002
In Tampa with Patrick

9:00 a.m.
Patrick and I are at the visitors center on MacDill Air Force Base. We have been granted the unbelievable opportunity to go on a refueling jet for an orientation flight. This whole day was arranged by friends from Scott Air Force Base at the request of General Handy himself. (I knew I liked him.)

11:00 a.m.
We've been introduced to General Hodges, who gave us an overview of the Air Force and also an idea of what to expect on the flight. We were also given the lowdown on safety procedures. It was a little disconcerting, but I feel confident that the flight and refueling mission will run smoothly. If the weather is any indication, we are in prime shape. The sky is perfectly clear.

3:15 p.m.
We've returned from the flight. It was an extraordinary experience. We were given the star treatment and allowed to sit in the cockpit for takeoff and landing. The big moment of the day was when the other plane approached us in preparation for

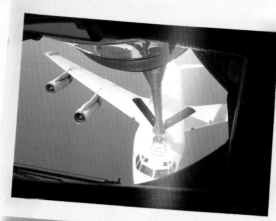

refueling. We went
to the rear of the
jet and were allowed to lie
down in the control space to see through the
window on the floor. Then they let Patrick and me raise and
lower the boom. It was a strange sensation. The control
handle was so responsive. I would move the control handle
only half an inch, but the boom would shift radically
outside. We got out of the way when the plane came within
sight. The plane kept coming closer and closer. I thought it
was close enough, thank you very much. I had to remind
myself that eventually the plane would stop, and indeed it
finally did, only 20 feet from our plane! That was a bizarre
sight—seeing the pilots from another plane so close we could
wave to them. The skill and precision exercised by this team
was incredible.

After the refueling was under way, Patrick and I retired to
the seats in the body of the plane and ate a box lunch. We
tried to talk, but the noise was deafening. We sat and
reflected on the marvelous experience. This was once in a
lifetime.

5:09 p.m.
After we landed, I stayed on the airfield to take pictures

and sign autographs. I handed out the rest of the Trading Spaces coins that I had given to the TS gang at Christmas. The airmen really appreciated them because they know the significance of the coins. Plus they knew they had something rare. No other airmen would have one.

*January 2nd, 2003
Still in Tampa

I met with the Enterprise Rent-A-Car people today to go over the particulars for the commercial I will be shooting for them tomorrow. I am thrilled that Enterprise wanted to use me in a commercial. And they have made it all extremely easy by setting up the shoot in Tampa (instead of New York or LA) so I wouldn't lose precious time with Patrick. We went over wardrobe options and discussed the story line for the spot.

Today was the first time I had seen a finished storyboard for the commercial. I had a few concerns regarding the story line, but Enterprise was very receptive to my suggestions. We all put our heads together and started brainstorming ways to make the commercial a better fit for my personality. The best idea called for a "husband" to be part of the story line. I hear from the other side of the room, "Well, is your husband available?" It never occurred to me we'd use Patrick as the husband, but it really did make sense. We were in Tampa, he's here, he's an actor, and fans across America already know him from A Wedding Story. Enterprise loved the idea. Next thing I know I'm asking Patrick, "Hey, Hon', how'd ya like to book a national today?"

Enterprise Shoot

6:00 a.m.

We are already on set for the commercial shoot. These shoots always start at the crack of dawn. The decision to use Patrick in the commercial happened last minute, so the verbal memo hasn't made it all the way down the chain of command yet. There seems to be rampant confusion about who Patrick is. Some people think he's the actor originally slated to be the "carpenter" in the previous story line. They keep trying to put him in work boots and a tool belt. Other people know he's playing my "husband," but don't know he is actually *my husband*. Still others know he's my husband, but they don't realize he's *the* "husband." They think he's just hanging out with me and they can't understand why he keeps milling about the wardrobe racks or why he's sitting in the makeup chair. Slowly everyone is clueing in.

Even though Patrick is a "husband" as opposed to the originally conceived "carpenter," the commercial still calls for him to be working on a home improvement project. They have him in the front yard of a house with sawhorses and an electric saw. I'm trying not to laugh, but if you knew my Masterpiece Theatre husband, you would know that this is a very unlikely scenario for him. It's just not his thing. But he looks so cute. He's doing a terrific job and I'm so proud of him.

12:00 noon

We've wrapped this half of the commercial, and it's on to the second location in front of a home improvement store. The other actors won't be needed for this half so I say adieu to Patrick. He will go home and take a nap. He's still got a show to do tonight!

*January 4th, 2003
Day 0

Today I'll meet up with my sister at the airport. For her birthday present I bought her a plane ticket to join me in Arizona for the Trading Spaces shoots. She is actually going to be a production assistant for all three episodes in Arizona. It's kind of strange that her birthday present is for her to come out and work, but she is psyched. She's a stage manager, so this stuff really turns her on. I'm just happy we're going to spend two weeks together.

The first episode is in Tucson, so we have a bit of a drive ahead of us from the Phoenix airport. The really cool thing is that my dad and stepmom, Katie, are coming to all the Arizona episodes too. They are taking advantage of Brooke and me being in the same place. It is so rare that the four of us are all together. I wish Patrick and Lu, Brooke's boyfriend, could be here, too, but it will be wonderful with just the four of us.

7:00 p.m.

Brooke and I arrived at the hotel in Tucson just in time to meet the whole gang for dinner to celebrate Edward's birthday.

When we arrived at the restaurant I saw that the large parking lot was completely full. I thought, "What moron decided this crowded restaurant was the perfect place to bring a group of 25 people?!" *Oh yes, that's the side of me I hate to show: the* impatient, annoyed, and intolerant side. Well, I don't know why I got myself in such a tizzy. The restaurant had a separate room that accommodated all of us. It was super! Jeff decided he'd order Rocky Mountain oysters – that's bull's balls for all you city folk out there. I consider myself pretty open to trying new things, but that just wasn't for me. Kudos to all the boys who gave it a shot.

★ January 5th, 2003

Day 1: University of Tucson, Arizona
Designers: Genevieve & Edward
Neighbors: Sarah & Sally and Matt & Ben

The funniest thing about today was the ongoing adventures of Man-bug (alter ego of a ladybug). Our sewing coordinator,

Daniel, strapped on some wings and antennas and flitted about in a delightful fashion. Fabulous entertainment.

*January 6th, 2003
Day 2

I don't really think about getting older that often. I feel young. My life is exciting. In a way it feels like my life is just beginning. But being around these college students has given me pause. When did I stop knowing the current lingo? When did the jargon become something I couldn't even decipher? Is 33 sooo old? I don't think so, but what the heck is "steez" and "slacked out"?! That's what Matt and Ben said when they saw their new room. They were slacked out and Edward had steez. Don't ask me. There you have it. I have officially crossed over to the adult dimension.

*January 10th, 2003
Day 2: Scottsdale, Arizona
Designers: Frank & Vern
Neighbors: Dana & Chris and Kari & Tom

If I had realized that my producer planned to shoot the Open on the grounds of our hotel, I would have given my dad more of a heads up. He and Katie were hanging out in my room when I called to tell him we were all out there if he wanted to come watch us shoot. I said, "I'm swinging around the back of the room; come out and hop in the car." My dad told me he didn't have on shoes or a shirt, but I said it was now or never. We were heading to Mummy Mountain behind the resort. My dad is stellar. Next thing I saw was my dad hopping over the wall of the patio with shirt and shoes in hand. He was like a superhero. As we peeled away to catch up with the caravan, he said, "Katie went for a walk. Hope she doesn't freak out when she comes back and I'm not in the room." We laughed.

© Marc Jeff Schirmer

© Marc Jeff Schirmer

* *January 11th, 2003*
Day 0

We went back to Mummy Mountain for the Open and Designer B-roll of this upcoming episode too. The photos tell it all.

Is this cool or what? Chocolate that looks like polished rocks!

*January 12th, 2003

Day 1: Scottsdale, Arizona
Designers: Doug & Frank
Neighbors: Stacey & Chris and Michelle & Jody

5:00 p.m.

Brooke and I are out of here! Cyndi, our location coordinator, is letting us go early for the day so we can make it to the basketball game. Cyndi, YOU ROCK!! Thank you so much! Brooke and I will meet the rest of the family there.

January 13th, 2003

Day 2

I gave the shirt that I wore in this episode to Stacey and Chris's teenage daughter. Yep, I'm somebody's best friend now.

Jan 12th

Ticket 1:

S0112
EVENT CODE
$95.00
123U
SECTION/AISLE
75X
ROW 32
SEAT 8
WA1622
10JAN3

PLATINUM CLUB
ROW/BOX 32 SEAT 8
2002-2003 NBA SEASON
PHOENIX SUNS
VS
UTAH JAZZ
AMERICA WEST ARENA
SUN JAN 12, 2003 6:00PM

ADULT
ADMISSION
95.00 PLATINUM

CN 53929
EWS0112
EVENT CODE
123U
CA438AWA SEC. 123U
32
95.00 ROW 32
SEAT 8

002625863931

EVENT DATE/TIME
SUBJECT TO CHANGE
NO REFUND
NO EXCHANGE

AMERICA WEST ARENA

Ticket 2:

S0112
EVENT CODE
$95.00
123U
SECTION/AISLE
CA
75X
ROW 32
SEAT 7
WA1622
10JAN3

PLATINUM CLUB
ROW/BOX 32 SEAT
2002-2003 NBA SEASON
PHOENIX SUNS
VS
UTAH JAZZ
AMERICA WEST ARENA
SUN JAN 12, 2003 6:00PM

I have been looking forward to this day since early December. My dad is a huge basketball fan, so when I knew he and Katie were going to be in Arizona with Brooke and me, I got Platinum Club seats for the Suns-Jazz game as a Christmas present for him. I had some difficulty arranging it, but I called for some help from a gentleman I met who works for the Washington Wizards. He put me in touch with some official Suns representatives, and I was able to finagle six tickets. Dad, Katie, Brooke, Ray, Val, and I are all going! My dad's favorite things: basketball and family. I know he's excited. Wait till he finds out there's a bar in the Platinum Club and he can order a Brandy Manhattan! He'll be in heaven.

*January 14th, 2003
Travel to Las Vegas!

4:32 p.m.
I'm here!

I can't wait to see the Bakers. Patrick and I were married in
their backyard, and they are the dearest of friends. They want
me to stay with them, but I think it will be good to have my own
space at the hotel. All of the cast and crew will be staying at
the Aladdin Hotel and Casino. I just got to my room and it is
fabulous! I have a king-size bed and a whole separate sitting
area on the other side of a rounded wall—so cool. My bathroom is
gorgeous, with marble, wall-to-wall windows, and an enormous
six-person bathtub. I don't know what I'm supposed to do with
that, but it sure is impressive. The window by my bed is floor-
to-ceiling and my view is of the Strip. I can see Mandalay Bay,
The Luxor, Excalibur, New York New York, and MGM Grand and its
huge videotron. And the pièce de résistance—I can see the
Bellagio hotel and the dancing fountains. If you have never
been to Vegas, I swear it would be worth the trip just to see the
Bellagio and the fountains. The streams of water are actually
choreographed to music, and the fountains go off to a different
song every half hour *(every 15 minutes at night)*. You have never
seen water shoot so high into the air. I could watch show after
show—it takes my breath away. Another great thing about my
room is that I can see Red Rock Canyon. I'm on the 32nd floor,
and there is nothing built across the street from the Aladdin,
so I have a clear shot all the way to the hills. The sun is
starting to set, and I can already tell it is going to be
painfully beautiful.

12:00 midnight

I did get to see the Bakers. We went to Olive Garden. I love Olive Garden almost as much as I love Vegas. Ahhh. The Bakers, Olive Garden, and Vegas—all in one day. *Life doesn't get much better than this.*

Tomorrow will be a very early morning because Hildi, Amy Wynn, Doug, and I will be doing in-studio radio interviews with all the morning radio shows. There will be a lot of press and media coverage over the next few days because of the whole LIVE thing.

*January 15th, 2003

Day 0: LIVE Episode

In addition to the Open and the Designer B-roll, we will be shooting the Key Swap today. We always shoot the Designer B-roll and the homeowner interviews on Day 0, but the Key Swap doesn't happen until Day 1. By shooting the Key Swap today, we will have everything on tape that the editors need to edit the first segment of the show. Normally an episode of Trading Spaces will come through postproduction in six to eight weeks. This episode will have to be edited in the two-day time frame so we can be ready for the LIVE Reveals. Anything we can do to help the edit team work faster and more efficiently will be a lifesaver. Sometimes we shoot projects out of order because it makes sense for lighting or location. For this episode we will shoot projects in the order they will appear in the show because we will be sending tapes to the producer, Aimee, and the editor, Jeff, throughout the day. As each tape runs out, it will go to the post studio for Aimee to log. *(That means notating each moment for reference during the editing process.)* It is the most tedious part of editing, but even in a time crunch it has to be done.

1:30 p.m.

We just had our production meeting to discuss the designers' plans and the technical aspects of the LIVE episode. Hildi's fabric for her room hasn't arrived yet. She's trying to decide

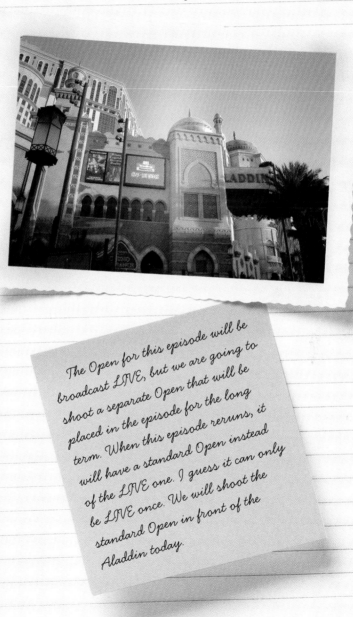

The Open for this episode will be broadcast LIVE, but we are going to shoot a separate Open that will be placed in the episode for the long term. When this episode reruns, it will have a standard Open instead of the LIVE one. I guess it can only be LIVE once. We will shoot the standard Open in front of the Aladdin today.

Dinner was splendid and so was our waiter, Phillip. I think this guy should have his own show. He was so entertaining—get this guy on camera.

whether she wants to change her plans or hope the fabric arrives tomorrow. She could be in quite a pickle if she doesn't have a backup plan.

4:00 p.m.

The Key Swap is finished, so I'm heading back to the hotel to rest a little bit before dinner. The Aladdin hotel invited Hildi, Doug, Amy Wynn, some PR people, and me to dinner at one of their restaurants, Elements. They even invited my parents to join us.

*January 16th, 2003

Day 1: Las Vegas, LIVE
Designers: Hildi & Doug
Neighbors: Caysi & Stephen and Kim & Jeff

Originally we were to go LIVE with The Early Show on CBS, but that got cancelled. I thought we were going to go LIVE with the local news affiliates at 7:35 a.m., but somehow that changed too, and I didn't get word. So I showed up at 7:15 a.m. in my makeup and wardrobe, ready to go, and nobody was here. The neighborhood was a ghost town. Crickets. The homeowners were still getting dressed, but Caysi and Stephen let me into the house so I could sit down and wait for everyone else to arrive. They were all coming at 8 a.m. In a way it was nice to just sit and rest. I made some phone calls back to the East Coast. It was like found money: found time. *Hey, I wonder how long that hour had been sitting in my coat pocket?!*

2:25 p.m.

Robin Leach came by the set and stopped over at Doug's house, but I missed it. I was working at Hildi's house. Darn. Apparently he was in leather pants, gave Doug some flack about ivory furniture, and brought less than "rich and famous" champagne.

3:00 p.m.

Some of the people who work on the TLC Trading Spaces website have been capturing all the events of the LIVE fury. They've been interviewing the designers, the homeowners, some of the crew, and me. They've even set up a video camera on-site so we can answer some of the fans' questions.

4:30 p.m.

Penn and Teller dropped by the set. They did a magic trick with Amy Wynn. I would have loved to have had a chance to talk with them a little bit, but they were in and out rather quickly. They were very slippery. I even had difficulty getting a picture of either one of them because they never stood still long enough for me to snap a photo. So consequently I have four odd nonpictures of Penn and Teller.

Day 2

11:30 a.m.

Rita Rudner is here. She is making a guest appearance on the show too. I love Penn and Teller, and Robin Leach was a nice touch, but I am thrilled to have Rita on the show. I am a huge fan of hers. I'm nervous to meet her because I'm afraid I'll act like a complete dork.

11:58 a.m.

Rita was awesome. She was even funny before she got in front of the camera. I wonder if she feels pressure to be funny constantly. She probably does, but I bet she is also naturally funny most of the time. She was such a good sport too. She is known for doing the splits, and she did the splits for us on camera. She's the best. I betcha Robin Leach wouldn't do the splits, even if he could.

3:34 p.m.

Elvis visited the set. I caught him coifing

his hair in the bathroom.

5:46 p.m.

The rooms aren't completely finished yet, and we still have two Designer Chats to tape, but we ran a rehearsal for the LIVE Open that will happen tomorrow evening. It will take place in front of Kim and Jeff's door. The LIVE crew is setting all the lights and they want to do a camera rehearsal. We will decide my exact spot in front of the house tonight, so there will be one less thing to concern ourselves with tomorrow.

LIVE

2:30 p.m.

I am getting really excited about the LIVE episode. Actually, I've been really excited about the LIVE Open. This will be the closest thing to theater I've done in a long time. One shot. Can't mess up. No option for a second take. Oh man, I love it. I've got butterflies in my stomach and I'm nervous and I'm jazzed. It feels like an opening night of a show.

4:45 p.m.

I quickly put on my wardrobe. This is the fourth day I'm wearing this outfit: first on Day 0, then Day 1, Day 2, and now the day of the LIVE Reveal. Eeeeew. Oh well.

We are going to rehearse the transition I will make from one house to the other between each Reveal. In the normal format of Trading Spaces there is a Designer Chat in each room before the Reveal. We taped these yesterday after the rooms were finished. So my chat with Doug will air while I get in place with Caysi and Stephen for the Reveal of their room. While the taped Designer Chat with Hildi is airing, I will be crossing the street to get in place with Kim and Jeff so they can see their new room. Caysi and Stephen will follow closely behind so they can be reunited with Kim and Jeff at the end. I will have about two minutes to be unhooked from the wireless transmitter (IFB) in my ear and one of the two microphone packs on my belt, cross the street, get in place with Kim and Jeff, and be attached to the wires in the other house. Denise will be in the satellite truck along with all the technical folks. They will communicate with me via the transmitter and wireless microphone. They will be able to see everything I do except when I cross the street.

Because I am the biggest klutz you will ever meet, the joke du jour with the cast and crew was that I was going to trip as I crossed the street and show up in the second Reveal with a broken nose or something. Knowing me, it's a probability. So as I crossed the street for the rehearsal, I made noises like I'd tripped and hurt myself. Immature I know, but I wanted to break the tension a little bit. Then I hear Denise in my ear through the IFB saying in a steady, even tone, "I know you're kidding and it's not funny." OK, OK. The rehearsal went well. No sweat.

5:34 p.m.
It's almost time to rock and roll.

1:34 a.m.
Wow! *What a night!* It was a real roller-coaster ride. We went LIVE at 6:00 p.m. in order to be LIVE on the East Coast at 9:00 p.m. The Open went well.

When the time for the Reveals drew closer, I headed back to the houses. We would reveal Doug's room first. Through the IFB I could hear the Designer Chat with Doug as it aired. Caysi and Stephen were brought into place with their eyes closed. It was even harder for them than most Trading Spaces couples because they had to be in place a little sooner. They had to keep their eyes closed for almost a minute as we waited for Doug's chat to end. They seemed nervous, and I tried my best to calm and comfort them as I listened for my cue. It was a lot of pressure for all of us.

In the final seconds, I contemplated what it would be like if they hated their room. I mean, what would they say knowing it was airing LIVE? What if they walked out? Would I try to get them back in the room? With only a couple of minutes of real time to juggle, I didn't know how much flexibility I would have. I just took a deep breath. I trusted that TLC would have never planned this whole LIVE event if they didn't think I could handle it. So with that, I heard my cue. I finally told Caysi and Stephen they could open their eyes.

My next task was to be completely in touch with every nuance of their reaction. Not only did I need to facilitate their opinion quickly, but I needed to be able to cut them off and dash away to the other house. Fortunately, Caysi and Stephen both loved the room. I let them discover everything they could and I pointed out a few things too. At the same time, I could hear Denise counting down in my ear. At 30 seconds, my antenna went up. At 20 seconds, I began listening for that perfect breakaway. At 10 seconds, I zeroed in. And at 5 seconds, I brought Caysi and Stephen's Reveal to a close and sent us to the other house. *I felt such a high. Honestly, I don't even remember what I said. I just know I did it!* I timed everything out perfectly. But I wasn't out of the woods yet. I still had to do the Reveal in the other house.

We crossed the street and did the same drill with Kim and Jeff. I got in place, then they got in place. I could hear the Designer Chat with Hildi. I tried to keep Kim and Jeff in the loop too. I told them to open their eyes. Again, a happy Reveal. Kim and Jeff loved the room Hildi and their friends had done for them. The couples were reunited on camera and again, I paid very close attention to everything going on. When I heard that 10-second warning, I closed the show and plugged an upcoming premiere of What Not To Wear, a new show on TLC.

I did it! Again, I couldn't tell you what I said, but I didn't miss a beat. I was on cloud nine! I did it! I actually did it! One of my producers congratulated me and said he knew of people who'd been in the business 20 years and couldn't do what I just did. I was really proud of myself. I couldn't even believe the happiness I felt. I exhaled a huge sigh of relief. Then I did a quick change into my cute little black skirt to go to the party.

After the press party, the cast and production team headed to Aqua, a restaurant in the Bellagio, for a more intimate celebration. We had just arrived at the restaurant, completely jovial and all aglow because of our amazing accomplishment, when my cell phone rang. It was my sister calling from Pittsburgh. She was in a bit of a panic and full of questions. She watched the LIVE airing of the show at 9:00 p.m. EST and even called to congratulate me and the team for a job well done. But now she was calling after seeing the repeat of the episode that aired at midnight EST—9 p.m. PST. She said something went wrong. I told her we were about to sit down to dinner. She said, "You don't understand. Something happened." I immediately put her on the phone with Steven Schwartz. I watched his face turn white.

He told us that the East Coast got the wrong feed from the satellite company at midnight. Instead of seeing the Reveals as they originally aired, they saw the camera rehearsal with the crew members as stand-ins. We wondered if that meant the West Coast got the same wrong feed at 9:00 p.m. PST, but fortunately, no—I called the Bakers and some friends in California, and they all saw the correct Reveal.

We found solace in the fact that the mistake was limited, but it was a real blow to our mood. I felt terrible for the TLC executives who worked so hard to make the LIVE Reveals a reality. It wasn't TLC's fault—it was a technical glitch with the satellite feed—but that didn't seem to offer the consolation they needed. We made jokes about the whole thing, but we didn't really think it was funny.

When we headed back to the hotel we saw the huge screen facing the Strip. It was showing clips of the Trading Spaces Reveals. It was surreal to see my face so huge on the street, but it was so awesome too.

January 19th, 2003
Day Off

9:04 a.m.

I'm up. I've been up. I've been trying to put away all the clothes I threw on the floor when I came back to my room and crashed on the bed. I was so exhausted from the adrenalin rush and hype of the LIVE Reveal, I didn't even wash my face before going to bed. How pathetic is that?

*January 20th, 2003
Day 0

We had a great time shooting the Open and Designer B-roll in the Aladdin Casino this morning. Wynn got decked out as a roulette dealer. It was fun pretending to gamble, because the casino set us up with the megachips. So Edward, Laurie, and I were betting $10,000 a hand for the shot. We imagined what it is like when the high rollers come out in the wee hours of the morning. It must be a different world at the tables when those guys start hitting the floor.

The B-roll took a little longer than I anticipated, so I was late to my photo shoot for Travel & Leisure. I met the photographer at the Bellagio because we were going to take the pictures in front of the dancing fountains. Dad and Katie met me there too. The article is for Travel & Leisure's back page appropriately titled "Just Back From." My page will be "Just Back From . . . Vegas." The photo shoot was an absolute blast. We had a PR person from the Bellagio call the control tower so the

172

dancing fountains would perform more often than their normal daytime schedule of every half hour. If we had to wait a half hour between every song, the photo shoot would have taken forever. So not only did the fountains go off over and over, but we were able to make requests! It was so easy to be enthusiastic for the photo shoot because I was having the time of my life.

*January 21st, 2003

Day 1: Las Vegas, Nevada
Designers: Laurie & Edward
Neighbors: Colleen & Jordan and Jesse & Rodney

There is a cement block wall that separates the backyards of the two houses. Jeff has found a way to prop himself up next to the wall so he looks like an owl. He's been hooting for the last ten minutes.

*January 22nd, 2003

Day 2

If I'm ever asked what has been the worst moment for me

on Trading Spaces, I have an answer. And any fan of the show will know exactly what I'm talking about, because it was all captured on camera and I can practically guarantee it will make the final edit of this episode. Here's what happened . . .

After getting the supplies ready to revamp a side table into an ottoman for Laurie's room, Aimee, our producer, set the action of the scene. Laurie would be predrilling holes on the side table, Colleen would begin cutting the foam cushion for the finished piece, and I would enter the scene to check the status on the project. Cameras were ready to roll when Laurie speaks up, "Y'all, is someone going to predrill these holes for me?" Aimee said, "No, you are going to do that." Laurie confessed, "I don't know how to do that, y'all." Aimee was stern, "Figure it out on camera."

We started the scene and all of a sudden I heard Laurie, with drill in hand, say, "It's smoking, y'all. It's smoking." I strutted over to Laurie with an air of superiority and told her she wasn't pressing hard enough to make the drill hole and she needed to put some elbow grease into it. With my tone, I practically implied that she didn't know what elbow grease was. I put my hands over hers and forced the drill into the table. Just then, the drill bit broke off into the table. I was mortified! Talk about karma! Laurie looked up at me. I stared back at her in shock and embarrassment. *You know, I've messed up projects before, but never after such a display of confidence. That's what made it so embarrassing.* I apologized, and Laurie and I started to laugh. Did I mention it was all caught on tape? I guess I did. Aw, man.

9:46 p.m.

I have fans of the show approach me all the time to tell me they "love it when the people hate it." Those fans will have a delightful surprise when this episode finally airs. If you thought "Crying Pam" from the fireplace episode was a handful, you haven't seen anything yet. This episode will bring "Angry Jesse" to the American public. I didn't see this coming. Jesse got mad that her room had been painted a color she doesn't like. She blamed the entire thing on Colleen and Jordan and is refusing to talk to them. I guess that cement wall between their houses is going to be built a little higher. I didn't know how to help her feel better. I was so sad that she was disappointed, and there was nothing I could say that made a difference. I felt even worse for Colleen and Jordan. They were at a loss.

After the cameras were turned off, Edward was able to talk to her. He tried to help her see she could repaint the room and like it very much. She tried to adjust to the idea.

The homeowners on Trading Spaces are almost always so thrilled with their new rooms that I sometimes forget there is a very real sense of jeopardy for our participants. I hope Jesse is able to come around and look back on her Trading Spaces experience with fondness.

*January 25th, 2003

Day 1: Las Vegas, Nevada
Designers: Genevieve & Vern
Neighbors: Bridgette & Kirk and Samm & Kenny

I completely forgot to mention the Archie comic book Kelle brought in to show us. Her mom collects them and her dad came across a very special one that spoofs Trading Spaces. It's called Betty and Veronica Spectacular: Betty and Veronica Are

Switching Places. It is a mock episode of Trading Spaces. They changed all the names of the cast, but it is so obvious who is who. I'm Perky. Ty is Toby, a rugged surfer-dude model-type. Doug is Darrell, with swooping bangs and a chiseled jaw. Amy Wynn is Annie. Dez is Helga, with a spiked blonde haircut. In the comic book they show Helga (Dez) getting a headache and having a breakdown. They show Darrell (Doug) storming out of the house after a tiff with Veronica. And Veronica is really putting the moves on the hot carpenter, Toby (Ty). My favorite line in the entire comic is when they're all finished. Perky (that's me) says, "Veronica bent the rules, though, going $8,000 over budget, but she agreed to cover those extra expenses herself."

✳ January 30th, 2003
In Los Angeles

This morning I made my third appearance on The Wayne Brady Show. It was a nice tie-in for me because they are doing an all-Vegas week. The set was decked out with slot machines and all kinds of Vegas lights and goodies. For my segment, they showed a clip of the "Paigetacular" musical number we used for the promo spot for the LIVE episode. Then I made my entrance wearing the exact costume I wore in the promo. I came out doing a showgirl-type walk. Wayne lost it. I got him to walk like a showgirl with me. I kept saying, "Lead with the hip. Lead with the hip." Like I know . . . please.

I talked about the LIVE Reveal experience. And I was even able to brag about our ratings a little bit. I mentioned that the LIVE Reveal episode was the highest-rated show ever on TLC and that we broke our own record. Trading Spaces now holds the top three highest-rated spots on TLC. I think the other two are the "Grave Blanket" episode and the "Natalie Maines" episode.

3:30 p.m.
I have been picked up by a car service to go to Long Beach for a Discovery event. I will be judging a video contest. The videos will be created for fun and laughter by groups of advertising and marketing executives.

The car service was originally going to drive me from LA to Long Beach, but the Discovery folks were afraid I wouldn't make

it to the event on time due to traffic.
The new plan . . . charter a private
plane. OK, whatever you say. Isn't this how
rock stars die?! Breathe, Paige. It's how musicians
die, not hosts. Last I heard of a host going down in a
plane crash . . . I've never heard of a host going down
in a plane crash. OK. So now the car service is
dropping me off at the Santa Monica airport, where I
will hop in a VERY small six-person plane and fly
to the John Wayne Airport in Long Beach.

My very small plane must be meant for six very
small people because it doesn't look like it can hold
my bag, let alone four other passengers. I'm glad I'll
be the only person besides the pilot.

5:23 p.m.
WOW!! That was amazing. I was a little scared, but
not enough to keep me from looking out
the windows. I couldn't
help

recalling my flight in the refueling jet at MacDill AFB. Once again I was in a cockpit, wearing headphones, and anticipating a takeoff. The quarters were much tighter this time, but thrilling just the same. Our takeoff was much smoother than I would have thought. The pilot figured all the coordinates by hand and without the assistance of complicated computers. Our runway sent us in the wrong direction, but that was OK with me because it meant we would be sweeping over and around Santa Monica. I could see Century City and the Hollywood sign in the distance. We flew right over Santa Monica Pier and headed straight down the coast. I even spotted the Queen Mary.

For such a short distance my flight was long—about 45 minutes—because we weren't going as fast as a jet. But I got to Long Beach on time and without the risk of running into highway traffic. What an experience!

*February 1st, 2003
Still in LA

I was getting my hair cut when the stylist asked me if I had seen the news that morning. The space shuttle exploded upon reentry. At first everyone thought it was terrorism because of the Israeli astronaut on board. But reports are coming out doubting that notion, and slowly NASA is investigating any problems with the aircraft. I think it was only natural for officials to think of terrorism first. September 11th really affected America and the world in such a lingering way.

I fly a lot and try hard not to dwell on that day when I'm at the airport or in a plane. But I have to say that something like this, even though reports are determining otherwise, puts the notion of terrorism right back in the front of my mind.

I remember so vividly where I was when I heard that the space shuttle Challenger had exploded in 1986. I was in class when some kid opened the door to the classroom and casually spilled the information. He expressed it with such little emotion that I thought he was making a morbid joke. I remember that it never once occurred to me that it could have been related to any form of terrorism (which it wasn't). But now that's our first thought. My, how times have changed.

Now I don't really want to fly today because I'm scared again, simply because I'm remembering September 11th. It's silly, I guess. I called my mom and told her I loved her. I didn't mean to be dramatic about it, but I wanted to touch base with someone before I flew. I'm off to Atlanta to visit Patrick for a couple of days before heading to Miami for some more Trading Spaces shoots.

*February 6th, 2003

Day 1: Miami, Florida
Designers: Kia & Hildi
Neighbors: Kim & Eric and Nancy & Rich

9:00 a.m.

We did a crazy Key Swap today. Larry had the homeowners in canoes as I handed them their keys from a pier. It was a creative way to include the lake that was behind their houses, and it added a little excitement to a part of our show that is often routine.

*February 7th, 2003

Day 2

11:07 a.m.

Last night the camera crew was going over the tapes for this

180

episode and discovered a technical problem with the footage for the Homeowner B-roll. (That's the same as the Designer B-roll: The neighbors are asked to do an activity that will play during my voice-over introducing them in the episode.) We are going to have to shoot it again. As far as TV is concerned, it's not such a big deal. Like I said, it's just a quick little shot showing them doing an activity together. I believe they are going to barbeque. It doesn't even involve sound because it will be covered up by my voice-over anyway. The problem lies in the fact that these couples are not supposed to see each other at all until the end of the challenge. For continuity issues they will have to wear the same wardrobe they wore on Day 0 when we did the interviews. Those clothes are not only dirty and need to be pulled out of the hamper, but the shoes they were wearing have paint on them from yesterday's work on the rooms. We can't allow the teams to see anything that would give away clues to what's happening in their own homes. This is going to be a tricky business.

The homeowners have obviously switched houses and can't go looking for their own clothes from Day 0. So Mindy and I rummaged through their hampers and closets to find the clothes they wore the other day. So pleasant. We had to think of everything—jewelry, belts, the color of their socks. Continuity can be a pain. A little spot remover to get the paint off their shoes, a little ironing to get the wrinkles out of their dirty clothes, and we had two sets of homeowners ready to reshoot their B-roll. Sure it was gross, but it worked. What can I say?

*February 9th, 2003

Day 1: Miami, Florida
Designers: Hildi & Laurie
Neighbors: Veronica & John and Anne & Gerald

7:00 a.m.

I wanted to work out this morning at 5:30 a.m., but the gym at this hotel doesn't open until 6:00 a.m. I didn't fret. I figured it might be nicer to walk along the boardwalk at the beach instead of using the treadmill anyway. So at 5:30 a.m. I headed out the door. Well, it's still dark out at 5:30 a.m., and I didn't feel safe walking alone along the beach. I told myself I was being silly for being afraid, but then I came across this guy dressed in a trench coat with gloves and a hat and heavy boots. It was early in the morning, but it was already 70 degrees outside! He was dressed way too warmly for the weather. My instincts told me he was up to no good, and my heart pounded faster as I tried to make it to a staircase that would take me off the boardwalk and back to the street. I was so afraid this guy would rape or kill me. Even after I made it to the street I wondered if he was following me, but he wasn't. I felt much safer on the sidewalk because there was a lot of traffic going by. So much for the spiritual walk by the ocean.

10:06 p.m.

I rode home from the set with Larry and Mindy, but we didn't get very far when we realized traffic was completely stopped leading up to the ramp for I-95 South. We didn't know what was going on at first because we couldn't see ahead of us on the highway. We could see the guy in the car next to us picking his nose, though. That was nice.

When we finally got up to the accident, we didn't see any cars, just one covered-up body. We wondered if the person had jumped from the highway level above ours. Maybe they were walking along the highway and got hit. Who knows, but that was definitely a dead body. Creepy. I got a little nauseous.

February 10th, 2003
Day 2

Oscar, a local grip who has been working with us on Trading Spaces, made a batch of Cuban coffee that was DELICIOUS. What a treat. This stuff is amazing. It is served like espresso, but it is stronger and sweeter.

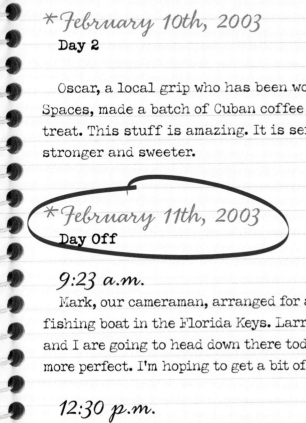

February 11th, 2003
Day Off

9:23 a.m.
Mark, our cameraman, arranged for a group of us to charter a fishing boat in the Florida Keys. Larry, Aimee, Ron, Wager, Mark, and I are going to head down there today. The weather couldn't be more perfect. I'm hoping to get a bit of a tan.

12:30 p.m.
It took almost two hours to get to the Keys from Miami, but we're about to board the boat. First we had to pick up sandwiches, snacks, and drinks for the day. **Gotta have snacks!**

We will be escorted by Captain Jack and his mate, Gilligan—just kidding—Ted.

1:00 p.m.
We pulled away from the dock. It is beautiful on the water. We all went to the bridge of the boat to watch as we powered out to sea. After we got a few miles out, we paused to catch our own bait. This is something I didn't know we would be doing. I just assumed we'd use nightcrawlers or something. Deep-sea fishing

183

Ron caught the first fish of the day. It was a massive struggle. It took over 20 minutes to get that darn fish in the boat. It was HUGE— at least 40 inches long! When he finally did reel the fish in, Ron got sick and threw up immediately.

is a whole different can of worms. (I'm so funny.) The fish we'll be going after are quite large and they need decent-size bait to get them to bite. We'll be using speedo fish. After we had enough bait, we traveled a little farther out to sea and dropped anchor about five miles offshore. Ted took care of the bait and set all our rods and hooks.

4:30 p.m.

Ron caught the first fish of the day. It was a massive struggle. It took over 20 minutes to get that darn fish in the boat. It was HUGE—at least 40 inches long! When he finally did reel the fish in, Ron got sick and threw up immediately. Everyone bet that I would be the first one to get sick on the boat, and I definitely felt queasy when that fish was caught, but I kept my lunch down. I didn't realize this fishing experience was going to be so violent. After Ron reeled the fish to the boat, Ted stabbed it with a big hook to bring it up into the boat. When it was on the deck, it was flopping around trying to breathe and bleeding all over the place. I suppose I'm a loser to admit this, but I never knew fish bled. I mean, when you cut a piece of rare steak it bleeds, but when you have sushi there's no blood. So when I saw that poor fish with blood running from its side, I felt so guilty and bad. I couldn't understand for the life of me why we were doing it. So instead, I sunned myself at the head of the boat while the rest of the group caught fish. I did wind up reeling one in. I only did it because of the peer pressure. I did not see the thrill in this sport. I called my dad and he was very proud of me and jealous that I was out there. My dad loves to fish and he loves the gorgeous blue water in the Keys. We threw back seven of the fourteen fish that were caught, but I still don't know why we bothered to keep seven of them. They were all huge: king mackerels and amberjacks. We can't take them back to our hotel.

Just when we were ready to head back to shore, we experienced one last thrilling moment. Wager caught a shark! My goodness. We threw him back too—the shark, not Wager.

Heading back to shore was my favorite moment of the day because the pelicans soared next to the boat and Ted fed them the leftover bait. The wingspan on these birds is at least six feet, and it was magical to see them glide so close to the boat. It looked like they were floating behind us.

5:45 p.m.

Well, there we were—the six of us and our fish. The tradition is to hang them in front of the boat to show off the day's catch. People were pretty impressed with our accomplishment. Other boats didn't have the success that we did. Captain Jack cleaned and prepped all our fish, and Ted invited us to his house to cook some of it.

11:54 p.m.

Ted's wife, Jennie, was so welcoming. She bagged up all our extra fish so it would be easier to give away, and she made a salad to go with the fish Ted was grilling. It was a relaxing evening and so nice to wind down after being in the hot sun. We called Oscar and had him meet us near his home when we drove back to Miami. We gave him all our fish. He'll freeze it and enjoy it. I'm just glad it won't go to waste. We told Oscar the only thanks we wanted was more Cuban coffee. He makes the greatest, sweetest, strongest Cuban coffee. If I didn't think my heart would stop from caffeine exhaustion, I would drink his Cuban coffee all day.

February 12th, 2003
Day Off

12:30 p.m.

I did an interview with ESPN, which seemed like an odd match.
Me, sports? The interview was about the adjustment teams have
to make after their home stadium has been remodeled. Does
remodeling have an impact on a team's record? Is there any truth
to one's surroundings having an impact on one's emotional well-
being and performance level? Absolutely. Why do you think
people react so strongly, positively or negatively, to the changes
we make in their rooms on Trading Spaces? Regardless of the
stylistic opinion of the decor in someone's room, the space holds
memories. If the space is tampered with, so are the items that
represent those memories. I said that maybe a new stadium can be
enjoyed by the fans and the tourists, but a stadium is a team's
home. Remodeling is going to have a direct impact on the
ownership the team feels for that space. They may feel like
visitors in their own home all of a sudden. The reporter told me
he thought my insights were interesting because, as it turns
out, statistics reveal that teams do suffer a dip in performance
after their stadium has been remodeled.

February 13th, 2003
Day 0

We shot the Open in the Florida Everglades. This was a
rousing experience. Larry arranged for us to be on the airboats.
These boats are the coolest things I've ever seen. They just skim
over the foliage that grows in the water. A regular boat would

get completely
wrapped up in vines
and get stuck.
These airboats were
powered by huge
fans above the water
so the vines could not get tangled
in the motors. And, boy, can those boats move
fast. Holy mackerel! The driver of my boat took off so fast the
cold air made my eyes water. The crew was in a separate boat so
they could shoot me cruising on my boat.

The second part of the Open involved using the resident
alligators at Everglade Holiday Park. Our producer wanted to
use two alligators in the shot for impact. The trainer implied
that we'd have impact all right—the impact of the big
alligator's mouth closing down on the little alligator's head.
"Big alligators like to eat little alligators" is what I believe
he said. That didn't stop Larry from asking if there was any
way to accommodate the request. As I held the 4-foot alligator
in my arms, the trainer told me to get directly behind the
6-foot alligator and stand in the big alligator's blind spot.
Since the 6-foot alligator would be unable to see the 4-foot
alligator, we would all be safe. Strangely, I wasn't scared at
all. I figured that the trainer would never take this "risk"
with me if he honestly believed I was in serious danger. I
suppose there was always a chance of getting injured, but I
trusted that the trainer believed the odds were in my favor.
Perhaps I should have been more concerned for myself, but I
love reptiles so I was actually very excited.

*February 14th, 2003

Day 1: Miami, Florida
Designers: Frank & Hildi
Neighbors: Adina & Alina and Rhonda & Paul

So right off the bat we have a problem. How to keep Adina and Alina straight in our heads? Adina actually owns the house so in my mind I dub her the head of the team. Also, Adina comes first alphabetically so I'll equate those two things. Otherwise I know I'll be asking all day, "Which one are you?"

Mindy, our AP, started our day off with love. She gave us all valentine cards and heart-shape boxes of chocolates and lollipops. Thank you, Mindy. We love you too. Kiss, kiss. I've sent flowers to Patrick—a dozen red roses. I thought it would be nice to go back to the basics, the classic choice. I did, however, add two white roses because it's a tradition for us to include them in the bouquets we send each other. In the past when I've had an opening night and there are many flower arrangements at the stage door, I could distinguish mine from the rest as soon as I spotted the two white roses. It's our little code.

10:35 a.m.

We just accidentally tripped the security alarm at Adina's house. Woohoo! Yep, I hear sirens. Nice. I wonder how far behind this will put us.

11:08 a.m.

Well, it was the fire alarm we set off, not the security alarm. The sirens I heard were from fire trucks. Apparently someone from the crew called to say it was a false alarm, but the fire department was obligated to inspect the situation anyway. The firemen were very sweet about the mistake. They even went on camera as they made their safety check. They were great guys. And cute. What is it about firemen? Hubba hubba.

6:02 p.m.

I spoke to Patrick. He thanked me for the flowers and told me they were beautiful. As I was saying good night he stopped me from hanging up to ask if I had received any flowers from him. I hadn't. He was so saddened by that news. He had gone to such lengths tracking down the address where I would be today, calling the Banyan production office to get the specific part of town, locating a florist in the area, asking Ron (our location coordinator) to keep a lookout for the delivery. I may not have the flowers in my possession, but I feel all the romance. It was just as much a surprise to hear it from him over the phone. I was so touched that he had gone to so much trouble. Patrick has always been very romantic. He was disappointed, but I was glowing. I love you, Honey.

*February 15th, 2003
Day 2

8:00 a.m.
The flowers from Patrick arrived yesterday after all! They came after Larry, Mindy, and I left for the evening. Patrick chose roses too—a dozen pink roses, with two white ones, of course.

*February 17th, 2003
In Atlanta with Patrick

Patrick helped me shop for wardrobe to wear when I tape Hollywood Squares next week. He was patient. Then we FINALLY saw the movie Chicago!!!! I can't believe it's taken me this long to see it, because I spent two years of my life doing the stage production on Broadway and on tour. It was worth the wait.

*February 18th, 2003
Travel to NYC

I love when travel becomes an adventure—not. The Eastern Seaboard has been experiencing dreadful winter storms, and the weather is causing cancelled flights and closed airports throughout the Northeast. I have not been spared delays on this trip. . .

I was trying to get from Atlanta to NYC for our appearance on the Today show. Matt and Katie are going to "trade" dressing rooms. Cool. My flight from Atlanta took off as scheduled, but my connection in Boston was cancelled. It was already 9:30 p.m.

when I landed in Boston, so my options were extremely limited. I looked into other airlines, I looked into taking a train, and I even tried the bus schedule. Nothing would get me into NYC in time to go LIVE at 8:00 a.m. I thought about renting a car, but I was exhausted and concerned I'd fall asleep at the wheel during the four-hour drive. I called Denise and asked what she thought about me hiring a car service to drive me into the city from Boston. She thought it was a great idea and added it would give me a chance to sleep on the way down. Fabulous plan! The folks at American Airlines in the Boston airport helped me track down a car company that offered such a service.

The driver was sweet, and I felt like I was in capable hands. We stopped for gas and even got McDonalds french fries. It felt like a childhood road trip, but it was hard to sleep because I was nervous about the driver getting sleepy. I dozed off and on and, at one point, awoke to flashing red lights from a police car. I thought maybe we'd been pulled over for speeding, but that wasn't it. It seems the police have had a big problem with drug trafficking between states in the northeast, and it is all happening with black Lincoln Town Cars and limos. When the police saw a Lincoln Town Car with Massachusetts plates driving through Connecticut at 2:30 a.m., they were suspicious.

My driver was the farthest thing from a drug dealer, but even my suspicions were alerted when he couldn't produce the registration for the car. There was some discussion about the license plates not belonging to the car either. I'm a big drama queen, so when the officer asked my driver to step out of the car I began to get a little nervous. They started rummaging through the trunk, and I ducked down in my seat. I didn't want to get hit by any stray bullets if a fight broke out. Oooooooh. Eventually the officer asked me to produce my ID. He took one look at my name and picture and said, "Oh geez, I don't believe this. I watch your show all the time. Well, you are clearly not drug trafficking. Where are you headed?" I answered, "Hopefully, New York by morning." They still gave the driver a ticket for the car not being properly registered, but they let him drive me to the City. Who knows what will happen after he pays the ticket. If I were in his place, I'd be steamed at my boss for letting me drive a car that wasn't registered. I finally arrived in my hotel room at 4 a.m.; I had to be awake by 6 a.m. to get into makeup for the Today show. Not easy.

The first day on the Today show went OK. Matt and Katie seemed excited, and their assistants have been busting their butts on the rooms. Matt called three times today, pretending to check on business with his assistant; he was no doubt hoping to scam some info about his room. Katie isn't coping with things any better. I think the secrecy is killing them! Hee hee.

*February 20th, 2003
Today show Trade

11:07 a.m.
NBC schemed with Doug for a fabulous practical joke. They've offered to cough up $2,000 to commission a faux Warhol of Katie to be placed in Matt's office. This is a brilliant idea! Even I can't be a stickler on the budget when it comes to a good joke. I can't wait to see Matt's reaction. It was his idea to hang pictures of Katie in her own office to make fun of her changing hairstyles through the years: Hair Today; Gone Tomorrow. This Warhol stunt is the perfect comeback.

12:08 a.m.
Earlier in the morning when we were all still at NBC, Amy Wynn got a phone call from her boyfriend saying her hotel room

Guess the caffeine isn't
working. . .
but Doug and Laurie
created beautiful offices for
Matt and Katie.

194

was flooded from a water leak in the ceiling of her closet. All her clothes were soaked. Well, when I finally got home this evening, I discovered water pouring from the ceiling in my closet too. Luckily, I only had a few articles of clothing hanging in there, but I hope none of them are ruined. The bellman helped me change rooms, and my things are being laundered. It was kind of a pain to change rooms, but the silver lining is that I now have a view of Central Park. Not a bad consolation prize.

*February 21st, 2003
Today show Trade

7:00 a.m.
Today we reveal the finished rooms to Matt and Katie. Somebody put bows on their office doors. It looks really cute. Everyone is excited and there is a lot of milling about. Doug is sitting in the makeup chair completely exhausted. It doesn't look like the coffee is giving him much of a boost.

9:46 a.m.
Matt's reaction to his new office was priceless. He buckled over with laughter when he saw the "Warhol" of Katie, and then he jumped up onto his desk to kiss it. Now that's great TV. He was very receptive to what Doug had done and he appeared to appreciate the effort and hard work. I'm not sure how Katie felt about her office. She was hard to read. I think she was a little overwhelmed and she seemed to be choosing her words judiciously so as not to offend anyone.

After the rooms were revealed, Doug, Laurie, Wynn, and I joined Matt and Katie in the studio for a final interview and wrap-up. All and all, I think the stunt was great.

PAIGE DAVIS

3:00 p.m.
I recorded some voice-overs for Trading Spaces and then I headed to Madison Square Garden to participate in a series of Westwood One radio interviews for Backstage at the Grammys. Dozens of DJs from across the country were set up to handle multiple interviews on location at the Grammys. I even went LIVE with some of them.

As I was walking from one table to the next for another interview, I heard a man break down into tears because he was so excited to see me there. I was unbelievably flattered by the intensity of his emotions, but I was also surprised because Carlos, a DJ known as Lita to his radio fans, appeared to be one of the least likely Trading Spaces fans imaginable. I'm not one to hold stereotypes, but people with bars pierced down the back of their neck, black gothic hair, and chains on all their clothing probably don't typically watch TLC. That's just a guess.

11:00 p.m.
I did a photo shoot for Good Housekeeping magazine at the studio where I take dance class in NYC. It was for a profile about my favorite things. I was a little insecure because it's

been so many months since I've danced, but it is, indeed, my very favorite thing and I wanted to represent that in the article.

After the shoot I stayed and actually took a class. It felt wonderful to be there again, but boy, I am out of shape. My dance teacher joked with me, "TV's made you soft." He's right. Sad, but true.

Tomorrow I fly to LA

February 23rd, 2003
Los Angeles, California

Today I taped Hollywood Squares. It was sooooo much fun. There were gifts galore in my dressing room too. I got a thick terry robe, a tote, a potable CD player, and a cute box of chocolates with Xs and Os.

I taped a week's worth of shows in one day—Monday through Wednesday before lunch, Thursday and Friday after. So I brought five outfits with me and changed clothes between each game. Howie Mandel was the "center square" and he was very supportive. He even helped me come up with a snappy joke for one of my questions.

It was stars on parade there, but my favorite was Charo. She was fantastic and funny but also genuine and real. Henry Winkler is an executive producer for the show and he made me feel welcome and comfortable. During the games I was picked often, so I got to play a lot, but I was bummed that I never got to be the "Secret Square"—something to aspire to. Sigh. Four friends came up from San Diego to watch in the studio audience, so the producers teased me for having a posse. The whole day was a blast. I can't wait to do it again.

*February 28th, 2003

Day 1: Orlando, Florida
Designers: Edward & Hildi
Neighbors: Carla & Brent and Jill & Craig

8:30 a.m.

I got ready extra early this morning so I would have time to do some radio interviews with stations in Atlanta. When I visit Patrick in a couple of days, I will be participating in a special cabaret performance by the cast of The Lion King to raise money for Broadway Cares/Equity Fights AIDS. I thought it would help generate ticket sales if fans of Trading Spaces knew I would be there doing a "meet and greet."

3:24 p.m.

Since the beginning of the season I've been taking an unofficial private count of how many people keep their toilet paper roll with the flap over and how many keep it under. I am surprised and dismayed to announce most people keep the flap under. Don't people realize this is just wrong? Hotels hang the roll with the flap over; they even fold the flap to a little point. It's the right way. I've been secretly turning the toilet paper rolls over if they are the other way. It's a compulsion.

*March 1, 2003

Day 2

The number of injuries I have inflicted on myself during these two days is out of control. I scraped my forearms as I carried out the old carpet from Hildi's living room, I wrenched

198

my thumb in the handle of a bucket, and I managed to give my fingertips second-degree burns when I was hanging the cording around Edward's ceiling. The worst part about the burns is I couldn't let out a scream as it was happening. As Carla and I were putting up the cording on one side of the room, Edward and Brent were taping a scene about the headboard on the other side of the room. Carla and I needed to be very quiet while we were working so we wouldn't bust the scene. We were using a hot glue gun to apply the cording and some of the glue was about to drop on the newly painted wall. I tried to save the wall by catching the HOT glue with my fingers. Hello, stupid. There I was with hot glue searing my skin and no way of ending the pain. I had to wait several seconds for the glue to cool down so I could pull it off. I opened my mouth in a mimed scream and managed to keep all the sound stifled. I was waving my hands in the air, and I was flailing my body around as I tried to channel the pain. Carla felt helpless; she didn't know what to do. Later she told me how impressed she was that I suffered so silently. And just when I thought that was the worst of it, I eventually peeled the glue off and pulled the skin on my fingertips right along with it. I have lovely blisters as a remembrance.

*March 3rd, 2003
Atlanta, Georgia

9:06 a.m.
I got here yesterday. It's nice to be with Patrick again, but we don't have much time to hang out with each other because there is a lot to do before the benefit tonight. I was able to do an in-studio radio interview at Q-100 to get the word out again. They

were very helpful and supportive, and I'm sure it helped. Those last-minute pushes can be vital to the success of an event like this.

Soon we will head to the nightclub for an all-day tech rehearsal.

2:08 a.m.

The benefit was a smashing success and I had a wonderful time. Patrick and I co-hosted the event, which showcased members of The Lion King cast doing their own thing. Many original songs were performed. There was a drag queen, a fashion show, and Patrick even did some magic. At intermission I led an auction for a special all-inclusive New York/Broadway weekend. I got the bid up pretty high as two men competed against each other. At one point, I enticed them to go higher with the bidding by promising to lift my skirt to expose the enormous, colorful bruise I had on my thigh from working on one of Hildi's rooms. It worked. The bid closed at $3,000. Turns out the guy who bid the highest heard about the benefit on Q-100 this morning. See, I told you those last-minute pushes can help. We raised over $12,000 tonight.

*March 7th-9th, 2003

Day 2: Los Angeles, California, Celebrity Episode
Designers: Genevieve & Vern
Neighbors: Andy Dick & Sara Rue

Andy loved his new kitchen. Sara was more than a little disappointed in her new office. It was a little tense around her house afterward. I wish I had known what to say to help her feel better. I really liked the office, though. I thought

Genevieve did a super job.

*March 13th, 2003

Day 2: Santa Monica, California
Designers: Laurie & Vern
Neighbors: Emily & Doug and Amy & Kristin

1:45 p.m.

Emily and Doug found out that Amy and Kristin caught a glimpse of an art project for their house. Unfortunately, Laurie's Gotlieb-inspired canvas was drying on the walkway and the ladies saw it. So much for the secrecy element of our show. The funny thing is that Amy and Kristin actually have a warped idea of what they saw. They seem to think that the canvas was of a cow or leopard print. They are now petrified that their room is going to be decorated in animal prints. Laurie's team decided to pack some decorative leopard print paper in a Fed Ex box and have it "accidentally" sent to Vern's room as a practical joke. The idea was for Vern to open the box in front of the two girls and then exclaim, "Wait. This isn't for my room. This is for Laurie's room." Now the girls really think Laurie and her team are doing animal prints in the room.

*March 14th, 2003

Day 0

I woke up this morning to my picture on the front page of USA Today. I was so surprised. Then I opened the paper to find a large, beautiful, color picture of me on the front page of the "Life" section. WOW!! It was a great article, highlighting TLC as a cable channel that has succeeded in developing a signature series for the network. <u>Trading Spaces</u> makes people stop on TLC in this day and age when folks have hundreds of cable channels to choose from. The picture kind of makes me look like the poster girl for cable networks. Cool.

I am so proud of TLC for getting recognized in this way. We have been set apart as an example. The industry is paying attention.

11:06 p.m.

Because we were back in LA for the celebrity episode, we were able to attend a dinner party thrown by previous <u>Trading Spaces</u> homeowners Jay and Rick from the Van Nuys shoot. It was wonderful to see them and Lisa and Teddy, who were on the other team. Jay and Rick kept their room basically the same. They rearranged the furniture to accommodate their TV, but that's about it. Lisa and Teddy kept their room EXACTLY the same. Like, for real, exactly the same—the artwork, the flowers, everything. They even carried the design into the rest of their

In Genevieve's room, the walls and air-conditioning units are leaking, so the paint won't dry. In the garage, the crew was faced with a nightmare: The leak in the roof was so big they had to place industrial-size trash bins in there to catch the water.

house. They took the stripe from the living room and extended it all the way to their front door, then added molding on the hallway cabinets to match the detail work on the wall unit we built for them. And get this: Teddy added indirect lighting to the open shelves above the wall unit. The room looks fabulous. I can't wait to tell Laurie how inspired they were by her work.

* March 15th, 2003
Day 1: Los Angeles, California
Designers: Frank & Genevieve
Neighbors: Robin & Josh and Michelle & Jason

10:07 a.m.
Well, just when we were counting our blessings that we haven't had to fight severe weather this season, we encounter torrential downpours today. This rain is unbelievable, and the problems arising from the weather are multiplying. The apartments are very small and cramped. In fact, we are so tight on space that we have rented a moving truck just to hold the furniture after it is unloaded from each apartment. There is no other place to put all that stuff. In addition to storing furniture outside the apartment, we were all counting on being able to shoot some scenes outside. But with this rain? That's not gonna happen. To complicate matters even more, we are dealing with leaks everywhere—some worse than others.

The crew set up the sewing equipment in the garage yesterday, but overnight the leak in the roof soaked everything. The teams neglected to tell us this could be a possibility. I'm not even sure they knew. The only saving grace was the designers' fabrics were not in the garage. But the special fabric-lined worktables were soaked and so was everything else. The crew had to execute an emergency transfer of Sewing World from the garage into the living room of a neighbor who lives in the same building as our teams. The teams' <u>Trading Spaces</u> shirts were also a wreck. A visiting producer pitched in and ironed the shirts in Genevieve's room while the crew transferred all that stuff.

Now the garage will be used for Ty's work space. This doesn't seem like a good idea either, but the crew has rigged a tarp to protect him from the leaking roof.

11:35 a.m.

Oops! The tarp in the garage didn't hold. It ripped and Ty is getting soaked. This day is unreal.

Fast Eddie ran to the store and picked up rain slickers, dry T-shirts, and socks for the crew. He is so sweet. The T-shirts have the **"As Seen on TV"** logo on the front. We all find this ironic, because none of the crew's madness will make it on TV.

* March 16th, 2003
Day 2

1:23 p.m.
OK, what happened to the rain? This is definitely a good thing and no one is complaining. But it does create a bit of a problem for our producer. We haven't shot the Open yet, but we have already shot the Key Swap, and in that scene it is pouring rain. It will look a little weird if I do the Open in the bright sunshine while the Key Swap *(which comes less than ten minutes into the show)* is in the pouring rain. Natalie came up with a clever idea: Because we saw on the news that heavy rain was possible for the day, she has written an Open in which I say the forecast calls for rain. It's true. So even though it's a bright, sunny day, I've got my raincoat and an umbrella. I'll let the audience know that rain is on the way. Boy, is it ever!

6:30 p.m.

This entire episode was plagued with one disastrous problem after another. The tight quarters, the typhoon rain, the leaking roofs and walls. It's a wonder we finished the rooms at all. But we did! And we even finished earlier than normal. To top it all off, our teams were thrilled with their new spaces. *Everyone do a little happy dance!*

* March 23rd, 2003

Day 1: Valencia, California
Designers: Laurie and Vern
Neighbors: Maggie & Ed and Laurie & Tom

9:00 a.m.

It's Key Swap time and I'm about to have my third encounter with a reptile this season. First Iggy the iguana from Long Island, then the alligators at the Everglades, and now Munch from Valencia. He is a monitor (a lizard that's related to an iguana).

Tom has quite a zoo: frogs, tarantulas, monitors, lizards of all kinds, snakes, and even cockroaches. This guy had to apply to the show, huh? Actually I really like reptiles. I'm looking forward to holding the monitors. And Larry is planning to incorporate them into the Open and the Time's Up.

* March 25th, 2003

In NYC

Tonight I attended an event for Discovery Networks and I got to meet Samantha Brown; she hosts Great Hotels on the Travel Channel. I was ecstatic when I heard she was at the event. I had to meet her! I love her and I'm a big fan. And I found out she

likes me too. We completely bonded when we met. We both found the only person with whom we could have a gripe session. I mean please, we've got the best jobs on the planet. How can we ever complain about anything?! Samantha and I understand each other's challenges in this wonderful yet crazy life that we lead.

*March 27th, 2003
In LA

1:00 p.m.

Well, I hit a record. Today I became the only guest to appear on The Wayne Brady Show four times. I just can't seem to stay away. I have such a good time on that show, and when they call, I run. I've bragged about Wayne before, so I won't gush, but he really is a remarkable talent. I think it's obvious to anyone who sees me on his show that I think he's the tops. This time on the show I promoted the Trading Spaces: Behind the Scenes book. We gave one to everybody in the audience.

8:35 p.m.

This afternoon I did a photo shoot for the cover of TV Guide. I had a blast at the shoot. We shot film for five different images. In

a few we went a little wild. By the end of the last roll of film, I was covered from head to toe in spackle!

* March 30th, 2003

Day 2: Los Angeles, California: 7th Heaven Cast
Designers: Hildi & Edward
Neighbors: Jessica & Beverly and George & Geoff

No one can doubt the efforts of our two celebrity women. Beverly is so exhausted she has fallen asleep on the floor while an entire closet is being built around her.

5:32 p.m.

Just when we thought the hard work was finished in Hildi's room, we ran into a big problem with the furniture, literally: The new sofa was too big to fit through the door. We tried everything. Even our associate producer, Kevin, was stumped, and he used to be a professional mover! Everyone was about to give up. We thought nothing short of a circular saw was going to help us get this sofa in the room. Then Kevin had the idea to lift the sofa through the window in the back of the apartment. OK. This idea was daunting at best because the apartment was on the second floor. But what other choice did we have? The sofa had to be carried all the way downstairs and around back. Kevin stood below the window, assessing the situation. The crew grabbed some rope and with a hefty heave-ho got that darn couch into the apartment. Success. Kevin, you're the master.

* March 31st, 2003

Travel

I'm on my way to Cincinnati to visit Patrick. The <u>Trading</u>

Spaces gear has to make the cross-country trek from Los Angeles to Orlando *(our next stop)*, so I have five days off to spend with him. **Glorious.**

* April 6th, 2003

Day 1: Orlando, Florida
Designers: Doug & Vern
Neighbors: Kelly & Angel and Julie & Kevin

8:00 a.m.

Julie and Kevin have left me a batch of peanut butter cookies. So clever. In the Newtown episode of Trading Spaces, Frank and I were painting wooden cookies for an art project. Frank wanted to paint chocolate chip cookies, but I tried to convince him not to, exclaiming, *"I don't like chocolate chip. I like peanut butter. Oooh, do peanut butter—you know, with the fork mark."* Trading Spaces fans remember everything.

* April 7th, 2003

Day 2

4:56 p.m.

Doug designed his martini room to be showcased at night. But it is still bright daylight outside, so the camera crew devised a way to make it look like nighttime for the taping of the Designer Chat and the Reveal. Here's a crazy behind-the-scenes tidbit for ya: They wrapped the entire outside of the sunroom with black plastic tarp. **Clever.**

* April 9th, 2003

Day 0

We shot the Opens in Disney World this morning for both this

The magic of television—it's broad daylight outside, but inside Doug's martini room, it's now nighttime, thanks to lots of black plastic!

episode and the last episode. The Open for the previous episode was pretty standard, but for this episode, our producer, Natalie, pulled out all the stops. Mickey, Minnie, Donald, Pluto, and Goofy all joined in the fun. I got chills down my spine when they showed up. It was extraordinarily special to see these characters skip toward us. With Cinderella's castle in the background and Disney music playing through the speakers along the walkway, I felt as if I'd been beamed back to Sunday nights and Walt Disney's The Wonderful World of Disney. Natalie ran to greet them. She started to cry. I think Disney touches a very deep place in many of us.

11:13 a.m.
Natalie will also shoot the Designer B-roll here, and we are all anticipating Hildi's arrival. She is a huge fan of Pluto. She named her dog after him, she has a Pluto collection, and she even incorporates him into her Trading Spaces rooms when she can get away with it. I can't wait to witness the moment she meets him.

11:34 a.m.
Hildi is here and she even brought a dog biscuit to give Pluto as a present. How cute.

* April 10th, 2003
Day 1: Orlando, Florida
Designers: Hildi & Frank
Neighbors: Jennifer & Dennis and Laura & Tim

10:03 a.m.
THIS IS MY 100TH EPISODE!!! I can hardly believe it. I was just watching the "Paint Reveal" in Hildi's room and I saw

Dennis paint a 100 on the wall. It's like a hidden salute. I giggled.

* April 11th, 2003
Day 2

12:23 p.m.

Natalie wants to do a scene with Frank's team in a kiddie pool. Seems like an easy enough task. Wrong. Our AP, Kevin, tried filling up the pool with water from the hose. But he felt it was too cold for Frank and his team to bear, especially since it wasn't very hot outside to begin with. Someone got the bright idea to get hot water from the faucets inside the house and add it to the pool. Next thing I knew, I was in an assembly line of crew guys running hot water from the bathroom to the pool. We tried to keep the flow continuous by gathering as many buckets as possible, but we hardly made any progress. Then we tried to hook up the garden hose to the showerhead. Great idea in concept, not great in execution. (Denise, maybe you should stop reading here.) Water spurted from the showerhead all over the bathroom floor. First Andy, our cameraman, held the hose to the spigot, and then Kevin gave it a try. Neither one of them succeeded in taming the water spillage. Plus, we were now running out of hot water, so it was a futile attempt. The guys settled for the kiddie pool being full enough. Natalie was pleased; that's all that matters. The end justified the means, I guess. I'm impressed that Kevin cared enough about the comfort of Frank's team to go to such lengths. He's a doll. He's nuts, but he's a doll.

3:12 p.m.

While Kevin was busying himself filling the pool, Eddie was

busying himself with a practical joke on Kevin. When the crew shoots the "BEFORE" footage of a room, Kevin lays down Xs on the floor to mark the exact placements of the camera. That way the camera can be in the same spots for the "AFTER" shots. It has to be exact *(they even take measurements)*; otherwise there would be a jump in the tape as it scanned from "BEFORE" to "AFTER" in the actual airing of the episode. Eddie decided to place Xs all over the room so Kevin would be confused—which X is the real X? Good one, Eddie!

8:23 p.m.

I just completed the Reveal for this episode. During my normal Close, "Thank you Hildi, Frank, and Amy Wynn. I'm Paige Davis, and that's another episode of <u>Trading Spaces</u>," the crew came into the room carrying a cake as big as a mattress. It had the <u>Trading Spaces</u> logo on it and read, "Congratulations Paige on your 100th Episode." I was flabbergasted. I started to cry. The homeowners congratulated me too, with a 100th anniversary Mickey Mouse watch. Whoa! And Chris, my dear friend and guide from Disney World, gave me a framed printout that said, "100 Shows of Paige."

It's mind-boggling to know I've actually done 100 of these babies. *(That's 30 cities, 200 rooms, 400 neighbors.)* It seems like only yesterday I taped my very first show.

* April 12th, 2003
In LA

I flew in this morning because tomorrow I'm going to be on <u>Celebrity Jeopardy</u>. My friends from San Diego even came up to visit and they are going with me to the studio. But today is just fun time—shopping, dinner, and, of course . . . champagne.

* April 13th, 2003
Jeopardy

11:09 a.m.
Well, it's over. I lost. I couldn't get that buzzer to work. Yes, I know everyone says that, and I am guilty of assuming it's just an excuse, but it really is tricky. At least it was for me. Whenever there was a break in the game, a swat team would form around my station with people giving me tips on how to finesse the buzzer. It was to no avail. Each time there was a question (or "answer" as is the case in Jeopardy), all the buzzer tips would clash inside my head and I wouldn't know which tip to pick. I stymied myself every time. It was so frustrating. At one point I lifted my buzzer high over my head and shouted out to the audience, "This! This is the hardest part about Jeopardy!!"
Serenity now!!!

12:37 p.m.
I'm on a flight to South Carolina. Tomorrow begins the 56th episode of the season. We're winding down now. I'm a little tired from the overnight trip to LA, but it was a great experience to be a part of Jeopardy. It is such a big part of American culture.

* April 14th, 2003
Day 1: Greenville, South Carolina
Designers: Laurie & Frank
Neighbors: Tracee & Brian and Julie & Steven

8:00 a.m.
I got peanut butter cookies again! This is getting funny. Julie and Steven were the elves.

9:40 p.m.

When I walked into my hotel room this evening, I was overwhelmed by the sight of two enormous vases, each filled with 50 roses. The owners of Banyan Productions sent me 100 roses to celebrate my 100th episode. **Wow!** Ever wonder what 100 roses look like? Well, now I know.

* April 15th, 2003
Day 2

10:23 a.m.

Today we let the crowd that had gathered on the street be in the background of the Open. They cheered for Greenville. It was a fun idea.

Aimee and Kelle sat up last night and made signs for the fans to hold, but then Aimee decided to let the crew guys hold the signs instead. They were insane out there. They screamed and cheered right along with the crowd as if they were born and raised in Greenville, South Carolina.

* April 16th, 2003
Day 0

12:08 p.m.

I began this morning with a few hours of a radio tour. This time the location was my bed. Gotta love radio. I hadn't even brushed my hair yet.

Now I'm heading to Duncan Park to shoot the Open. Larry had Trading Spaces baseball jerseys made for the designers and me. Larry put the number 0 on the back of Doug's shirt. *Hee hee.*

3:43 p.m.

When I arrived at Duncan Park, I saw the entire Spartanburg

team on the field practicing for a game. A part of me loved having them there because it added to the ambience of the park. Another part of me was nervous because I had to do my Open in front of them. They watched as I made a fool of myself trying to catch a baseball in my glove. I was pathetic. It took me several tries. I could tell they were holding back their laughter. Oh gosh, how embarrassing. But hey, in TV you just have to capture it once—and I did, twice even. Ha.

10:30 p.m.

This evening I had the wonderful treat of spending Passover with some local families in Greenville. When Kenny Fried, a publicist who assists TLC with press, knew he would be in Greenville over Passover, he called the local temple and asked if they held a Seder. They didn't, but pointed Kenny in the direction of four families that gather together every year and could potentially accommodate more heads. Kenny, Mindy, and I took them up on the invitation. And it was a good call because it was a delightful and special Seder. These families are so close. And I'd never been to a Seder where someone played trumpet for all the songs. It was a beautiful and spiritual night.

April 17th, 2003

Day 1: Spartanburg, South Carolina
Designers: Doug & Edward
Neighbors: Lena & Niel and Kristin & Andrew

This is Carter's second episode as our carpenter. He's doing really well. Already he's getting a better handle on things and he's so adorable. He has stolen everyone's heart. The women are swooning, and the guys think he's great too.

Because there have been so many fans on the street during our episodes in South Carolina, Carter has been put into the thick of things right away. He never watched Trading Spaces and I don't think he quite grasped how loyal, devoted, and crazed our fans can be. He felt a little overwhelmed. I promised him that it wasn't like this every time. In some cities we won't see a single person on the street. In other cities we have hundreds of fans coming out of the woodwork. It just depends. He was taking it all in stride.

* April 22nd, 2003
Day 1: Downingtown, Pennsylvania
Designers: Genevieve & Vern
Neighbors: Becky & Bill and Betsy & Chris

8:00 a.m.
We're in the final stretch of the season. Only three more episodes to go, and they are all being shot in high definition. I think it's pretty exciting that we're having another opportunity to do that. The colors will look brighter; the fabrics will look richer. It makes me want a high-definition television.

11:34 p.m.
The partners at Banyan Productions arranged for the Trading Spaces/Banyan Productions folks to see a Phillies game from a luxury box at Veterans Stadium. I almost decided not to go because we finished at the houses so late and I knew I would miss most of the game. But the lure of being with my friends was too strong. A group of us jumped in the car and met up with the rest of the gang for the last three innings. Sitting in the box was great, especially since it was so cold outside. And the Phillies won too. Phillies 6, Rockies 3.

* April 24th, 2003
Day 0

12:00 noon

I just did another radio tour to publicize the Trading Spaces: Behind the Scenes book. This one was about five hours long, but I had some time between a few of the interviews. I called Patrick on each one of my breaks. We had our conversation in 10-minute intervals. It was kind of funny. We laughed at the absurdity of it all. People are always asking me how we make our marriage work when we are apart all the time. This is a perfect example of how we do it.

* April 25th, 2003
Day 1: Ambler, Pennsylvania
Designers: Hildi & Laurie
Neighbors: Debbie & Scot and Ellen & Scott

8:08 a.m.

These teams are fun. Scott is wearing a shirt that says, "Whose idea was this anyway?" It is one of four fun things the teams wore when they were originally scouted for the show.

10:09 a.m.

We've taken the idea of starting off with a bang to a new level. Our PA, Matt, just dropped the mirrored leaf of the dining room table as we were unloading Hildi's room. Crash! Now there's broken mirror all over the walkway to the front door. Way to go, Matt. Smile for the camera. I think we would all be more disturbed about the situation if we hadn't known that Ellen and Scott wanted to get rid of that table anyway. Sigh of relief for us and especially Matt.

* April 26th, 2003
Day 2

11:05 p.m.
Have we got an episode for all those people out there who say, "I love it when they hate it." Debbie and Scot loved the bedroom Laurie did for their girls. But as they predicted, Ellen and Scott were appalled by the dining room Hildi designed. It was a daring design, and Ellen was definitely not prepared for the bright yellow and black. She was very angry. Everyone asks me how I deal with it when people are unhappy with a finished room. The truth is I don't know how. I feel strongly about the rules of the game, one of which dictates that the homeowners have no say in what happens in their own room. But I am also sensitive to the homeowners when they are disappointed. Let's face it, if you're on Trading Spaces, you're hoping to get a fabulous room that you absolutely love. You're not really thinking about the risk part. My husband likens it to going on a game show. You don't go on a game show thinking you could be zoinked; you go on thinking you could win a brand new car.

Ellen definitely felt zoinked. There was nothing I could do or say. She wanted to take the room apart right away. She immediately started taking things out of the room and off of the walls. She was very clear that she hated the light fixture Hildi designed. She was definitely going to take it down and throw it away. Our cameraman, Rob, asked if he could buy it from her. She let him take it for free. That's the crazy thing about this show—a light fixture that's a nightmare for her is a fantastic steal for him. That's why when a homeowner is upset, I can never state whether or not I think it's a bad design. In the end, it all boils down to individual opinion. I guarantee you that for every room on our show, there are people out there who like it and people who hate it. I just try to listen and hope that I can convince them to live with the room for a few days before changing it. Sometimes it just takes time to get used to something new. For two days I thought the design for Hildi's dining room was nuts, but when it was finished, I kind of liked it. Actually, I liked it a lot. I got used to it and was won over.

* April 27th, 2003
Day Off

Today I flew to Cincinnati to surprise Patrick for his birthday. I knocked on the door of his apartment with balloons in hand. He couldn't believe it. We're having a wonderful time. I fly back tomorrow on our Day 0.

* April 29th, 2003
Day 1: Philadelphia, Pennsylvania
Designers: Hildi & Kia
Neighbors: Amy & Michael and Gabriel & Lee

8:00 a.m.
I put my TV makeup on in my hotel room because the crew and I shot the Open before heading to the location. Larry arranged for us to shoot the Open at Pat's Steak in South Philly. Because I prefer a vegetarian diet, Larry and I thought it would be funny for me to try to order a tofu cheese steak. The guy behind the counter did such a great job with the shtick. He played along brilliantly. Oooh, I smell an Emmy.

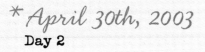

Today is our last day of shooting for Season Three. We are commemorating it by destroying that @#%&* Number III pillow that has plagued us for every episode. The pillow started out as part of a contest. "What, besides Paige, is in every episode of Season Three?" The contest never came to fruition, but the producers still had to find a place for the pillow in each episode—for posterity, our executive producer said. Whatever. We're burning it.

* May 1st, 2003
Last Entry

Tonight we celebrated the achievement of another season. This kind of event always makes me want to cry. We said good-bye to our dear boss and friend, Denise Cramsey. She's off to produce a show of her own creation. We wish her well, but we will miss her terribly. I'm actually still in denial. I couldn't bring myself to hug her—I just knew I'd lose it. One of her final duties included putting together a reel of memories and bloopers from the season. We all watched it at the party. She did a great job. It was funny, touching, and full of surprises—just like our season.

Doug brought the whole evening to a climax when he serenaded us with his own rendition of Sinatra's famous hit "My Way." His friends worked on the lyrics for months. It was hilarious, and he brought down the house.

I didn't want the evening to end. I know I have another season to look forward to, but things will be constantly evolving in the coming year. We've already added Carter to our family. Soon we will be adding a designer or two and another host. *Yes, another host. TLC is going to let families "trade spaces" in a Sunday evening version of the show.* My schedule cannot handle another 45 episodes on top of the 60 I already do, so they're bringing in a different host for the family episodes. That's gonna be weird for me, knowing people are trading spaces and I'm not there. But if there's one lesson I've learned by observing the homeowners on our show, it's that the people who have the best experiences are those who are able to embrace change and go with the flow. I'm excited to see the family show come together. I know kids across the country are going to be thrilled at the news. Up until now, you had to be 16 years old to participate on Trading Spaces. Not anymore. *Parents beware.*

It's been quite a ride this season. I'm sitting in my hotel room trying to make sense of it all. Each day I've been writing about little things and big things. And somehow they've all linked together to form an amazing journey for me and for our show.

Denise,
Steven
Schwartz,
and me

Trading
Spaces is
bigger than ever.
Our popularity has
skyrocketed in ways none of
us could have anticipated.
Our show has almost taken

on a life of its own with the
press and fans and media.
We have affected an entire
genre of television and set
the bar very high for the
imitators out there.

And at the root of it all,
one thing remained
constant . . . . We still had
homeowners, designers, and
carpenters working to put
together rooms in two days'
time with a budget of only

$1,000. And I was there
witnessing it all.

"...but

through it all,

I took the

chance

and painted

walls

in

leather

pants..."